Light & Fun!
Easy Puzzles and Brain Games

INCLUDES WORD SEARCHES, SPOT THE ODD ONE OUT, CROSSWORDS, LOGIC GAMES, FIND THE DIFFERENCES, MAZES, UNSCRAMBLE, SUDOKU AND MUCH MORE

LOMIC BOOKS

D1377132

Light & Fun!
Easy Puzzles and Brain Games

By Editor of Easy Puzzles and Brain Games
ISBN: 978-1-988923-01-7
Lomic Books
Kitchener, Ontario

Copyright

Disclaimer

Feedback and More Books

Your feedback is appreciated. To share your comments or questions

email: jmorend@lomicbooks.com

Are you interested in more puzzle books similar to this one?
Then check out:

www.lomicbooks.com

TABLE OF CONTENTS

INTRODUCTION

Welcome to *Light & Fun! Easy Puzzles and Brain Games* This entertaining book is filled with fun puzzles, brain games and trivia challenges.

In particular, this book has been created to offer the solver many benefits including:

1. A Terrific Variety of Puzzles

This book has over twenty-five unique styles of puzzles and brain games, providing the solver with a wide variety of activities to enjoy. Also, the different kinds of puzzles and games are evenly distributed, so no one type of puzzle dominates the book.

2. Exercises Many Mental Skills

*Light & Fun! Easy Puzzles and Brain Games*is is divided into four sections to maximize the mental skills that the solver uses to work on the puzzles and brain games. In particular, there are *Visual Puzzles* that challenge the solver's attention to detail; *Word Puzzles* that focus on recalling and expanding vocabulary; *Logic & Number Brain Games* that focus on problem solving; and *Memory & Trivia Challenges* that provide a fun way to work your short and long-term memory.

3. Comfortable to Work Through

With large print and clear pictures *Light & Fun! Easy Puzzles and Brain Games* is built to be easy on the eyes. This puzzle book is about doing fun mental games, not eye strain. To make looking up answers easy and convenient, under each puzzle or game is the page on which you can find its solution. Moreover, the solutions section is designed so that the answers are both easily readable and understandable.

4. Lots of Fun

The best part of *Light & Fun! Easy Puzzles and Brain Games* is the hours of fun that you can have working through the book. Whether you decide to pick and choose your puzzles — or work through the book from front to back — entertaining puzzles, brain games, and trivia challenges await.

With all of its great features, *Light & Fun! Easy Puzzles and Brain Games* is meant to provide you with a terrific puzzle experience. Please have a wonderful time working through the book.

Enjoy!

VISUAL PUZZLES AND BRAIN GAMES

- ✓ MAZES
- ✓ SHADOW FINDER
- ✓ SPOT THE ODD ONE OUT
- ✓ FIND THE DIFFERENCES
- ✓ PICTURES TO SAYINGS
- ✓ AWESOME ARRANGEMENTS

Maze

Find the path that goes from start to finish.

START

FINISH

SPOT THE ODD ONE OUT

Find the picture that is different from the rest.

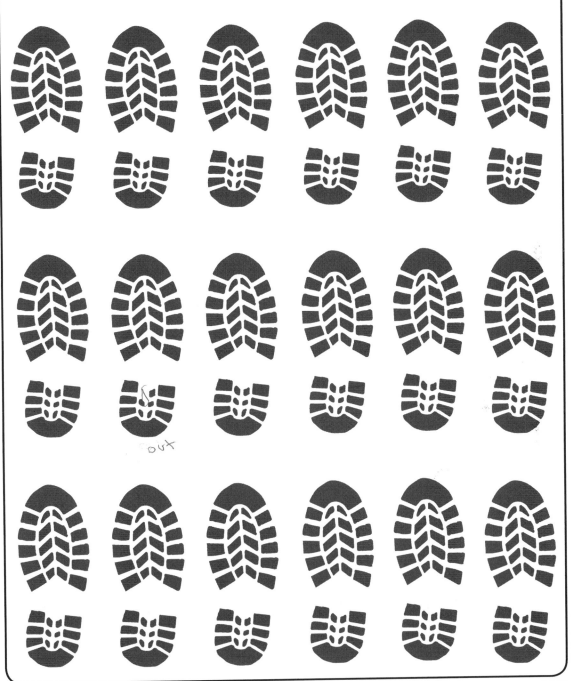

Solution on page 170

FIND THE DIFFERENCES

FIND 5 DIFFERENCES BETWEEN THE TWO PICTURES.

SHADOW FINDER

FIND THE SHADOW THAT FITS THE PICTURE PERFECTLY

PICTURE

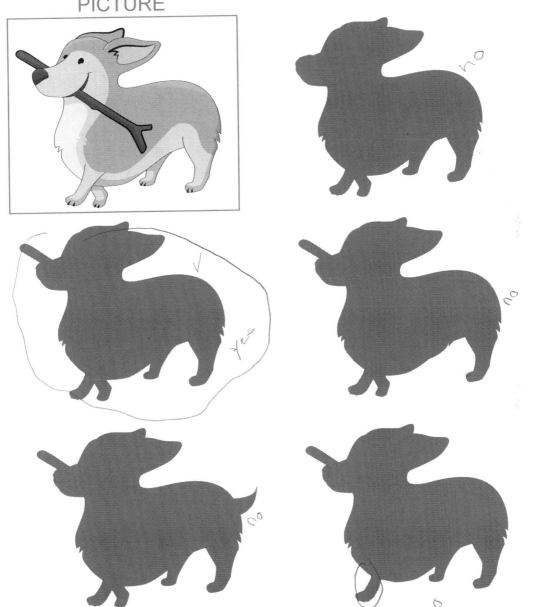

Solution on page 170

Pictures to Sayings

Use the pictures to figure out the common saying that is being represented.

Puzzle One

Answer: _____

Puzzle Two

Answer: _____

AWESOME ARRANGEMENTS

U SE THE WORDS AND THEIR VISUAL ARRANGEMENT TO FIGURE OUT THE COMMON SAYING THAT IS BEING REPRESENTED.

PUZZLE ONE

Answer: _____

PUZZLE TWO

Answer: _____

Solution on page 170

Maze

Find the path that goes from start to finish.

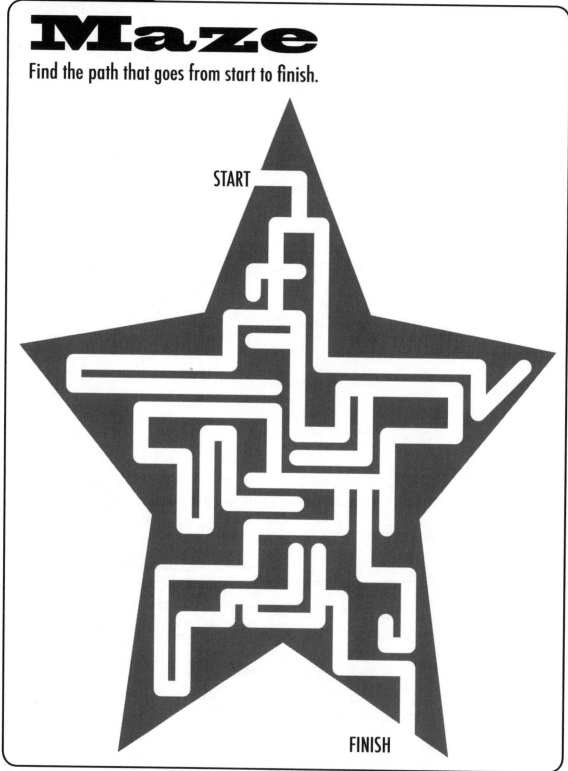

START

FINISH

SPOT THE ODD ONE OUT

Find the picture that is different from the rest.

Solution on page 171

FIND THE DIFFERENCES

FIND 5 DIFFERENCES BETWEEN THE TWO PICTURES.

SHADOW FINDER

FIND THE SHADOW THAT FITS THE PICTURE PERFECTLY

PICTURE

Solution on page 171

Pictures to Sayings

Use the pictures to figure out the common saying that is being represented.

Puzzle One

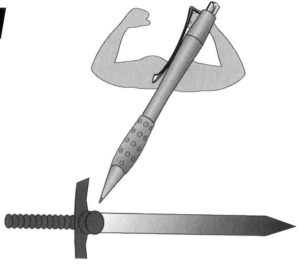

Answer: _____

Puzzle Two

Answer: _____

Solution on page 171

AWESOME ARRANGEMENTS

USE THE WORDS AND THEIR VISUAL ARRANGEMENT TO FIGURE OUT THE COMMON SAYING THAT IS BEING REPRESENTED.

PUZZLE ONE

Answer: _____

PUZZLE TWO

STICK Wrong

Answer: _____

Solution on page 171

Maze

Find the path that goes from start to finish.

START

FINISH

-20-

SPOT THE ODD ONE OUT

Find the picture that is different from the rest.

Solution on page 172

FIND THE DIFFERENCES

FIND 5 DIFFERENCES BETWEEN THE TWO PICTURES.

Solution on page 172

SHADOW FINDER

FIND THE SHADOW THAT FITS THE PICTURE PERFECTLY

PICTURE

Solution on page 172

Pictures to Sayings

Use the pictures to figure out the common saying that is being represented.

Puzzle One

 =

red, light, interesting, unusual, tv, noise, music, soft, golden, performance, actor, role, award, unusual, announce, comet, wide, loud, theatre, goodness, producer, trophy, appreciation, art, paint, news, fun, carpet, curtain, rug, ruin, stain, wild, coffee, tea, sugar, pop, plate, spoon, table, one, two, three, four, five, six, seven, eight, nine, ten, sparkle, dull, computer, internet, keyboard, screen, bag, container, pail, shovel, beach, sand, green, blue, chair, sit, stand, crouch, wonder, ponder, sing, write, paint, sculpt, glue, describe, sketch, draw, creative, alot, blue, sparkles, hello

Answer: _____

Puzzle Two

Answer: _____

AWESOME ARRANGEMENTS

USE THE WORDS AND THEIR VISUAL ARRANGEMENT TO FIGURE OUT THE COMMON SAYING THAT IS BEING REPRESENTED.

PUZZLE ONE

Answer: _____

PUZZLE TWO

Answer: _____

Solution on page 172

Maze

Find the path that goes from start to finish.

START

FINISH

SPOT THE ODD ONE OUT

Find the picture that is different from the rest.

Solution on page 173

FIND THE DIFFERENCES

FIND 5 DIFFERENCES BETWEEN THE TWO PICTURES.

SHADOW FINDER

FIND THE SHADOW THAT FITS THE PICTURE PERFECTLY

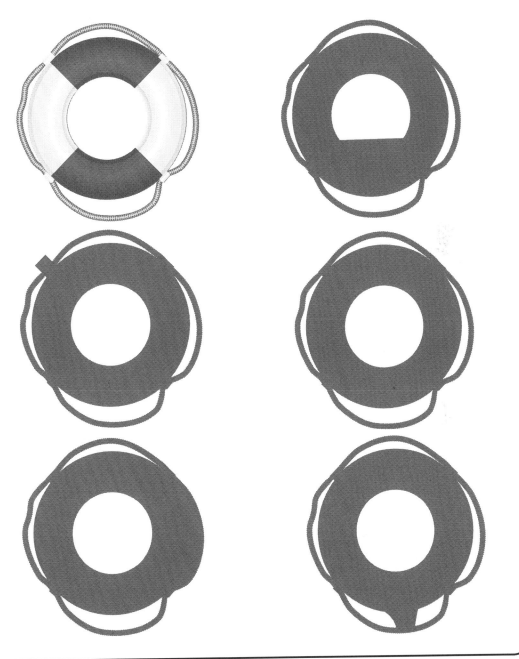

Solution on page 173

Pictures to Sayings

Use the pictures to figure out the common saying that is being represented.

Puzzle One

Answer: _____

Puzzle Two

Answer: _____

AWESOME ARRANGEMENTS

USE THE WORDS AND THEIR ARRANGEMENT TO FIGURE OUT THE COMMON SAYING THAT IS BEING REPRESENTED.

PUZZLE ONE

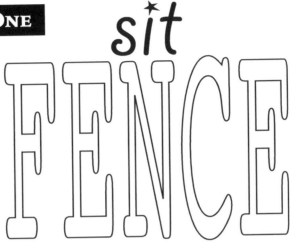

Answer: _____

PUZZLE TWO

Answer: _____

Solution on page 173

Maze

Find the path that goes from start to finish.

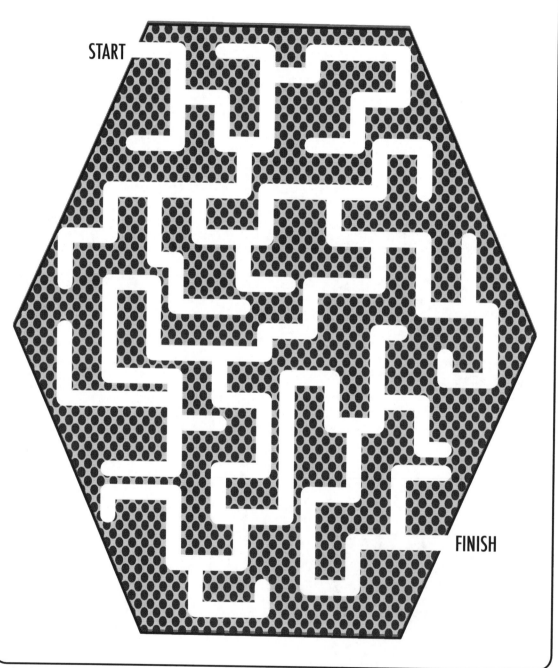

START

FINISH

SPOT THE ODD ONE OUT

Find the picture that is different from the rest.

Solution on page 174

FIND THE DIFFERENCES

FIND 5 DIFFERENCES BETWEEN THE TWO PICTURES.

SHADOW FINDER

FIND THE SHADOW THAT FITS THE PICTURE PERFECTLY

PICTURE

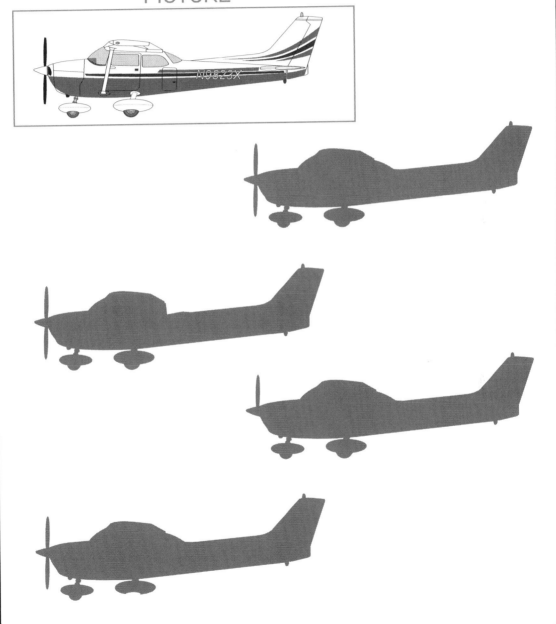

-35-

Solution on page 174

Pictures to Sayings

Use the pictures to figure out the common saying that is being represented.

Puzzle One

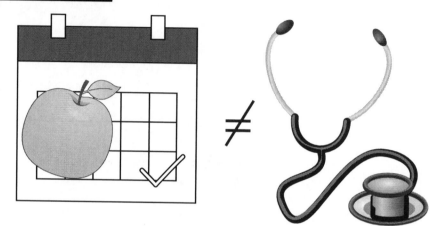

Answer: _____

Puzzle Two

Answer: _____

AWESOME ARRANGEMENTS

U SE THE WORDS AND THEIR VISUAL ARRANGEMENT TO FIGURE OUT
THE COMMON SAYING THAT IS BEING REPRESENTED.

PUZZLE ONE

Answer: _____

PUZZLE TWO

Jump
BANDWAGON

Answer: _____

Solution on page 174

Maze

Find the path that goes from start to finish.

START

FINISH

SPOT THE ODD ONE OUT

Find the picture that is different from the rest.

Solution on page 175

FIND THE DIFFERENCES

FIND 5 DIFFERENCES BETWEEN THE TWO PICTURES.

Solution on page 175

VISUAL PUZZLES

SHADOW FINDER

FIND THE SHADOW THAT FITS THE PICTURE PERFECTLY

PICTURE

-41-

Solution on page 175

Pictures to Sayings

Use the pictures to figure out the common saying that is being represented.

Puzzle One

Answer: _____

Puzzle Two

Answer: _____

Solution on page 175

AWESOME ARRANGEMENTS

USE THE WORDS AND THEIR VISUAL ARRANGEMENT TO FIGURE OUT THE COMMON SAYING THAT IS BEING REPRESENTED.

PUZZLE ONE

Answer: _____

PUZZLE TWO

BUD (with *PINT* vertically between the U and D)

Answer: _____

Solution on page 175

Maze

Find the path that goes from start to finish.

START

FINISH

Solution on page 176

WORD
PUZZLES
AND
BRAIN GAMES

- ✓ **WORD SEARCHES**
- ✓ **UNSCRAMBLE**
- ✓ **CROSSWORDS**
- ✓ **STARTS WITH**
- ✓ **DELIGHTFUL WORDS**
- ✓ **CLUES & RHYMES**

WORD SEARCH...
COFFEE OR TEA?

Find the words below in the letter grid to the right. Words may be hidden in an across, down, or diagonal direction. Also, the words may be spelled forwards or backwards.

WORD LIST:

BEANS	ESPRESSO	POUR
HOT	CAFFEINE	WATER
DRIP	ROAST	SERVE
LATTE	PRESS	HERBAL
GOURMET	GROUND	CAFE
FILTER	BREW	HONEY
MOCHA	BEVERAGE	BLACK
BREAK	LEAVES	POPULAR
MILK	SUGAR	INSTANT
CREAM	STEEP	DRINK
PERCOLATE	CUP	SOCIAL

```
P I H C A F F E I N E V I J P P M
P N K S Z F W E R B A C F P I R D
Z S D E D A P S A R S N K Q M D K
P T R N I Z K E B E A N S X Z X A
E A N Z U N R R P P L E A V E S B
R N B N I O E V P R E S S B I H S
C T Y R Z D R E M X P B O K G C O
O X D I D S D G Y C J S C Y P Y S
L Q R H S T E E P O X K B O P L S
A I U D F W D C D D G W P M U O E
T P S N I Q H G Y H D U O P O K R
E T T A L T X P Y P L C A Z E T P
Q G B N T S X N T A H B R V G R S
X R P F E A Q O R A S G Y J A N E
V K F M R O H M L U R J E E R L H
L T I I F R N K G F T T Z F E J E
M Q K C B M L A L T T E D A V F R
Y N F R A K R K V A M G M C E B B
E L U E V A S C P M I L K R B R A
N H R T M E D A N L J C T C U P L
O C D A O R H L U X X J O O N O A
H M R W J B P B S Q G X P S Q Q G
```

-47-   Solution on page 176

UNSCRAMBLE
NEWSPAPERS

In this puzzle, the goal is to create words from the scrambled letters that relate to newspapers and their content. Every letter is used to make each word. Put one letter into each square.

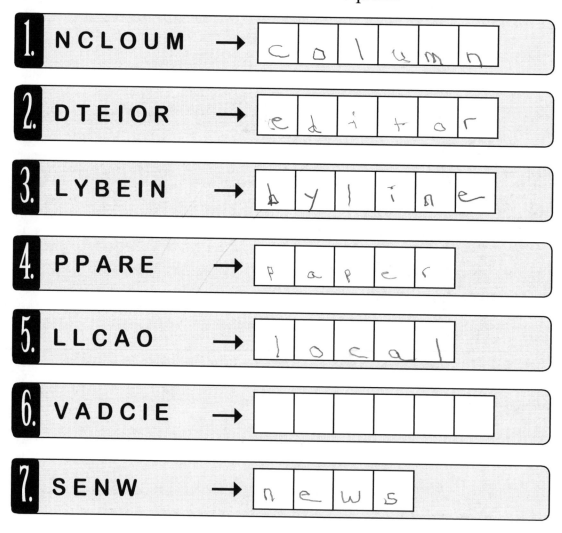

1. NCLOUM → c o l u m n

2. DTEIOR → e d i t o r

3. LYBEIN → b y l i n e

4. PPARE → p a p e r

5. LLCAO → l o c a l

6. VADCIE →

7. SENW → n e w s

8. CCMOIS → ⬚⬚⬚⬚⬚⬚

9. DEEARR → ⬚⬚⬚⬚⬚⬚

10. HPUILSB → ⬚⬚⬚⬚⬚⬚⬚

11. FIORNM → ⬚⬚⬚⬚⬚⬚

12. SSPROT → | s | p | o | r | t | s |

13. DAS → | a | d | s |

14. EEFAURT → ⬚⬚⬚⬚⬚⬚⬚

15. WEEVIR → | r | e | v | i | e | w |

16. ORSTY → | s | t | o | r | y |

17. CRLETAI → ⬚⬚⬚⬚⬚⬚⬚

Solution on page 176

CROSSWORD

In this puzzle, write the answer to each clue in the crossword grid. One letter goes into each square.

ACROSS

1) Another name for autumn
4) Group of musicians
8) An almond, for example
9) A great pilot
10) Return on investment
11) A type of tree
13) Kind, thoughtful
14) Lights the earth
16) Absolutely not
17) Veto
18) Swine
20) Mother
21) Outdoor swinging bed
24) Used to boil potatoes
26) Computer intelligence
27) Container or vase
28) Not moving
29) A group of twelve
31) Places to put cars
35) Yellow fruit
37) Elongated square

DOWN

1) Pieces of information
2) A playing card
3) Opposite of followed
5) Creative work
6) Opposite of yes
7) Supper
8) A familiar, pet name
12) Faster than a jog
15) Opposite of day
18) An upbeat kind of music
19) Opposite of big
22) Automobile
23) Nice
25) Opposite of in
27) Two of ___
28) Sweetens food
30) Takes care of children
32) Part of a play
33) Droop
34) Beer
36) ___, myself & I

Crossword grid (handwritten answers, 13 columns):

1 F	2 a	3 l	l	■	4 b	5 a	6 n	7 d	■	8 n	u	t
9 a	l	s	■	■	10 b	r	o	i	■	i	■	■
11 s	r	d	e	12 r	■	t	13 n	i	c	e		
e	■	■	u				c	■	k			
14 S	u	15 n	■	16 n	c	y	e	r	■	17 n	i	x
	■	i	■	s						a		
18 p	i	g	■	19 s			22	23		20 m	o	n
o	■	21 h	a	m	m	o	c	k	■	e		
24 p	25 o	t	■	a			26 a	i				
	u			l		27	u	r	n			
28 s	t	i	l	l			s	■	29 d	o	z	e	30 n
u	■											a
31 g	a	r	32 a	g	e	33 s	■	34 a				n
a	■		c			a		35 l	e	36 m	o	n
37 r	e	c	t	a	n	g	l	e	■	e	■	y

Starts with "P"

In this puzzle, the solution to each clue begins with the letter "P." You can write your answer in the blank space provided.

1. A meal where each person contributes something.

_____

2. Used to making jumping out of a plane safer.

_____

3. A writing utensil that includes wood and lead parts.

_____

4. An instrument that includes strings and ivory keys.

_____

5. Bird that has bright, beautiful feathers that can make a fan shape.

_____

6. Location where horses or cows can graze on grass.

_____

7. Tiny stones that can be found in a river or beach.

_____

8. To legally forbid a particular action or activity by law.

_____

9. A cucumber that is put in a brine of vinegar, water and salt.

_____

10. A person who you call when your pipes are clogged.

_____

11. A soft pace to put your head when you want to go sleep.

_____

12. The study of motion, energy, and the nature of matter.

_____

13. A black and white bird that lives in a very cold region.

_____

14. A person who provides commentary on politics or other topics.

_____

15. A structure that was built by the Egyptians as a tomb.

_____

16. The human organ that produces insulin for the absorption of sugar.

_____

17. To get ready for a trip or other significant task.

_____

18. A tropical fruit that has a tough exterior and waxy leaves on top.

_____

Solution on page 177

Delightful Words

Try to create ten words from each group of letters. You do not need to use every letter in each word. However, you can only use the letters that are displayed once per word.

Letters	Letters	Letters
u n s l b a	i t g f o z	y r c a e m

Words	Words	Words
an	gift	
sun	fit	
bun		
ban		

Clues & Rhymes
Quote and Quit

The answers to each clue in question one will rhyme with "quote." In question two, all of the answers will rhyme with "quit." You can put your answers on the blank lines provided.

QUESTION ONE: Answers Rhyme With "Quote."

A) A kind of bag
tote

B) Lay on top of water
Float

C) Animal that has horns
goat

D) Expand or puff up
_____

E) Helps you stay warm
coat

F) What Hemingway did
wrote

QUESTION TWO: Answers Rhyme With "Quit."

A) Weave yarn with needles
Knit

B) Just a little
bit

C) A group or set of things
_____

D) Keeps a hand warm
_____

E) Narrow opening
_____

F) To break apart
_____

Solution on page 177

WORD SEARCH...
THE SYMPHONY

Find the words below in the letter grid to the right. Words may be hidden in an across, down, or diagonal direction. Also, the words may be spelled forwards or backwards.

WORD LIST:

VIOLIN	WAGNER	CHORUS
TRUMPET	MOZART	PERFORM
PICCOLO	CLARINET	CONCERT
CYMBALS	ENSEMBLE	STRINGS
HARP	PIANO	FLUTE
CELLO	SONATA	MUSIC
BACH	BRASS	CLASSIC
SCORE	HAYDN	TUBA
VENUE	OBOE	HANDEL
RHYTHM	ALLEGRO	SCHUBERT
HORN	DRUM	CONDUCT

```
U X E O L L E C D T M C L L X D R
V E L B M E S N E C Y M B A L S M
Y J Q S O S C O R E N G A W X M E
T R U M P E T W H F W I X T C F P
T F M E K B U W W N N D Y A H M C
C E H U U S C H U B E R T C U G C
U V S R B V L J X F B O O S D N Q
D Z Q A Q V U K K H W Z I U R R J
N T C E T U L F C C G C G M U O R
O H B T H N J F L J V Q A F M H C
C O N C E R T F A I E N S S A R B
T L X C V R U F R H N Z D I R G A
F O R G E L L A I L U V M S J D H
H C J H T I Z J N T E I R D U L V
A C F G B O E S E M Y O O F B G M
N I S A S B J V T A V L F L C D Z
D P U T C G A O B O E I R R I I T
E O R E R U N T N D C N E Q S O U
L N O T X A B I A B S J P P S G B
T A H W E I Z B R N A I R O A S A
H I C B H N Q O M T O P A H L L K
P P R H Y T H M M V S S H Q C A A
```

Solution on page 178

UNSCRAMBLE
WILD WEATHER

In this puzzle, the goal is to create words from the scrambled letters that relate to the weather. Every letter is used to make each word. Put one letter into each square.

1. UHTNERD → ☐☐☐☐☐☐☐

2. EAGL → ☐☐☐☐

3. EEEFRZ → ☐☐☐☐☐☐

4. LHIA → ☐☐☐☐

5. CCYNEOL → ☐☐☐☐☐☐☐

6. ORSTM → ☐☐☐☐☐

7. LFODO → ☐☐☐☐☐

8. WOSN ☐☐☐☐

9. YTOHOPN ☐☐☐☐☐☐☐

10. AQUSLL ☐☐☐☐☐☐

11. XHEUMDI → ☐☐☐☐☐☐☐

12. LOCUYD → ☐☐☐☐☐☐

13. ELEST → ☐☐☐☐☐

14. OORNTAD → ☐☐☐☐☐☐☐

15. SUTG → ☐☐☐☐

16. ODRUTGH → ☐☐☐☐☐☐☐

17. OOONNSM → ☐☐☐☐☐☐☐

Solution on page 178

CROSSWORD

In this puzzle, write the answer to each clue in the crossword grid. One letter goes into each square.

ACROSS

1) Characteristics
6) Tennis serve that isn't touched
8) Associated Press
9) Very
10) Opposite of rich
12) Tear apart
13) Something a horse eats
15) They ground a tree
17) Can use it to bake cookies
18) Make money
21) Very fancy light fixture
23) A long time _____
24) Use it to hear
26) Small fabric covering
28) Standard no. strokes in golf
29) The two of us
31) Brings attention to
34) Have property rights
36) Move legs quickly
39) Goes with 'either'
41) Green light
42) Blue and red mixed
45) Opposite of he
47) The jig __ up
48) Say it when you leave
49) Unscrambled information

DOWN

1) Opposite of near
2) Majestic story
3) You and me
4) To decompose
5) Use it to eat soup
7) Feline
11) Every _____ has its thorn
14) Curly haired dog
15) Opposite of fake
16) Get ready for a trip
19) Found in chicken soup
20) Use it to take pictures
22) A kind of tree
25) Rodent
27) One plus one
28) An oblong fruit
30) female sheep
32) Sense of self
33) Not smart
35) Automobile
37) Not pretty
38) Opposite of yes
40) Grain used to make whiskey
43) Employ
44) Light-emitting diode

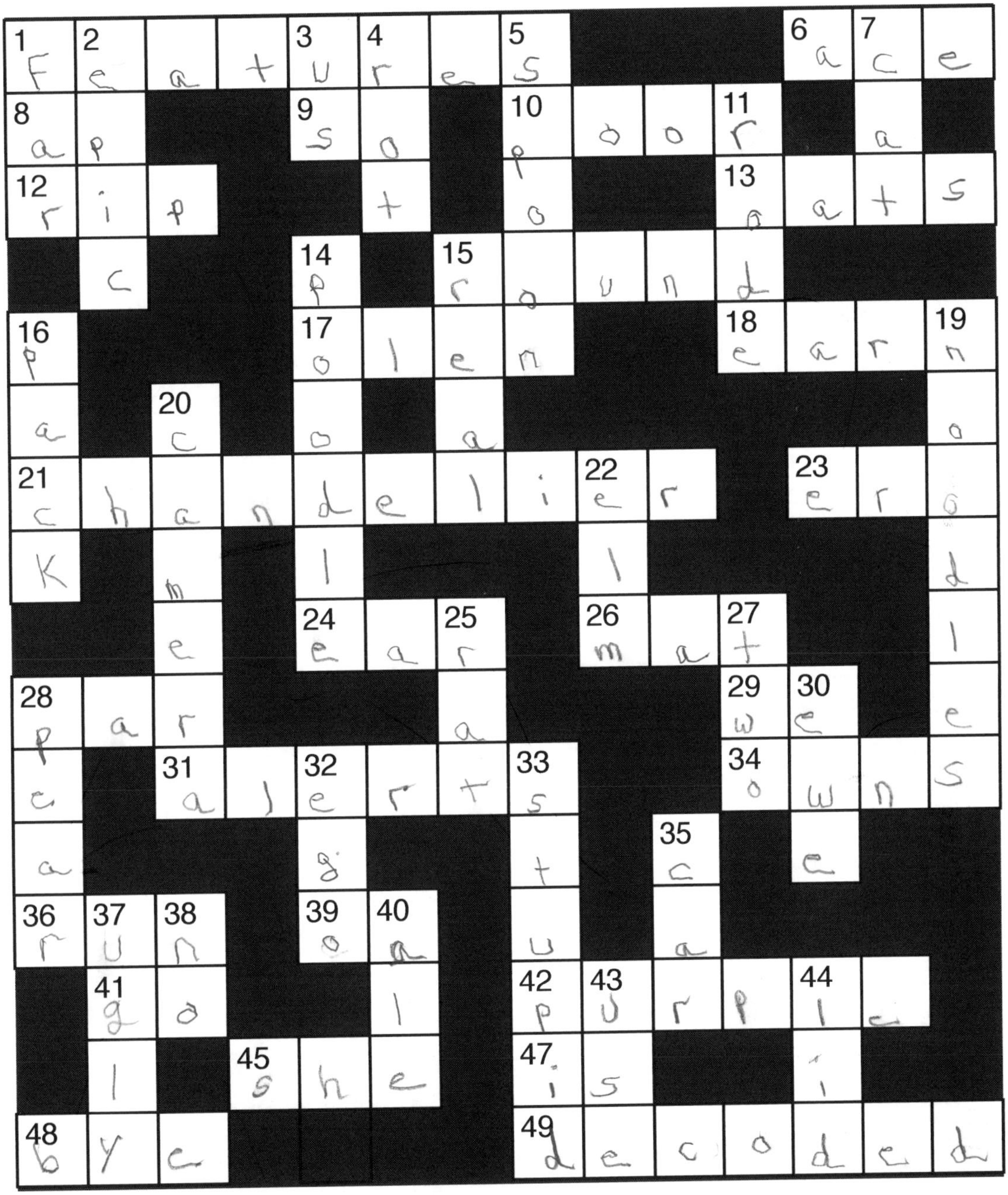

Solution on page 178

Starts with "U"

In this puzzle, the solution to each clue begins with the letter "U." You can write your answer in the blank space provided.

1. It can protect the person who carries it from the rain.

_____

2. The current of the water below the surface.

_____

3. All of the planets, stars, comets, moons and everything in between.

_____

4. Provide new, relevant information on an old news story.

_____

5. The official who make the call during a baseball game.

_____

6. When something is important, and needs to be addressed soon.

_____

7. A person who helps people to their seats at a show or wedding.

_____

8. A fork, spoon, knife or other hand-held tool used in the kitchen.

_____

9. A magical horse-like character that has a single horn.

_____

10. A description of something that has no value or utility.

_____

11. Common a hairstyle for women in a wedding or other formal event.

_____

12. To bring together a broad range of things or ideas.

_____

13. To inspire or improve a situation emotionally or otherwise.

_____

14. The characteristic of being genuinely different.

_____

15. The second or higher level of a house or building.

_____

16. Way to describe city life, as compared to rural life.

_____

17. An ideal, visionary, or imagined place where all goes well.

_____

18. When two sounds or notes are at a perfect pitch.

_____

Solution on page 178

Delightful Words

Try to create ten words from each group of letters. You do not need to use every letter in each word. However, you can only use the letters that are displayed once per word.

Letters	Letters	Letters
p t u v a r	c g o w t e	j l n a e s
Words	Words	Words
_____	_____	_____
_____	_____	_____
_____	_____	_____
_____	_____	_____
_____	_____	_____
_____	_____	_____
_____	_____	_____
_____	_____	_____
_____	_____	_____
_____	_____	_____

Clues & Rhymes
Free and Found

The answers to each clue in question one will rhyme with "free." In question two, all of the answers will rhyme with "found." You can put your answers on the blank lines provided.

QUESTION ONE: Answers Rhyme With "Free."

A) An afternoon beverage

tea

B) Has a trunk and leaves

tree

C) Pollinates flowers

bees

D) A big shopping trip

spree

E) Grows in a pod

F) Charge or cost

QUESTION TWO: Answers Rhyme With "Found"

A) A breed of dog

B) A noise

C) To strike many times

D) Land, earth or soil

E) The shape of a disk

F) Baseball pitcher's spot

Solution on page 179

WORD SEARCH...
SCIENCE FICTION

Find the words below in the letter grid to the right. Words may be hidden in an across, down, or diagonal direction. Also, the words may be spelled forwards or backwards.

WORD LIST:

STORY	IDEA	ORWELL
SPACE	ALIEN	WELLS
CONFLICT	WORLD	ASIMOV
ADAMS	THEORY	GAIMAN
TRAVEL	FUTURE	STAR
CLARKE	SCIENCE	IMPACT
TIME	PLANET	ROBOT
DARK	WARP	SHIP
DETAIL	GALAXY	CONCEPT
LIMIT	NEW	GENRE
VERNE	FANTASY	LASER

```
T H E O R Y S T K T D L A S E R D
J C D P A M I I V J I L G G V L E
Z O V I D E A M Z F P J L N O T T
V N C W Z R Y E R W Z I D E O E A
C C J X A S I M O V H R H B W C I
V E M M U S X V E R N E O S A R L
B P X E T U B D Y W A R V V W L O
P T D O T M D L R O W O E W Y I V
F V R V P D A R K N C R C A Y M A
N Y W W D R E M R I L I A C H I D
Y P I Z M V A X P Q A E P O N T A
E X G R V G Q W R W R S N A P M M
H H Q G T C A P M I K N L F Y Q S
T W K Q W E K X A W E E C L W Y L
A M Y Y E D N O B I T G Z I V S F
H Z Y N A M I A G X H E A C B A Y
B P Q L E E A H L X L C E T E T X
T R F E X I I Z S P U N R P A N A
Q M I V Q X L R L B C E U I C A L
N W M A R V A A L M V I T Z Z F A
I E W R N T Y T E A L C U P U C G
J N G T S I X A W O G S F V O M T
```

Solution on page 179

UNSCRAMBLE
MATHEMATICS

In this puzzle, the goal is to create words from the scrambled letters that relate to mathematics. Every letter is used to make each word. Put one letter into each square.

1. D A D → ☐☐☐

2. E E R C N T P → ☐☐☐☐☐☐☐

3. M S U → ☐☐☐

4. B N M U E R → ☐☐☐☐☐☐

5. G A L E A B R → ☐☐☐☐☐☐☐

6. E A G N L → ☐☐☐☐☐

7. R N T I G E E → ☐☐☐☐☐☐☐

8. RUFOLMA → ⬚⬚⬚⬚⬚⬚⬚

9. RAIOT → ⬚⬚⬚⬚⬚

10. IVIDED → ⬚⬚⬚⬚⬚⬚

11. KRABTEC → ⬚⬚⬚⬚⬚⬚⬚

12. EZOR → ⬚⬚⬚⬚

13. CFATRO → ⬚⬚⬚⬚⬚⬚

14. AAVEEGR → ⬚⬚⬚⬚⬚⬚⬚

15. EDMAIN → ⬚⬚⬚⬚⬚⬚

16. RHGPA → ⬚⬚⬚⬚⬚

17. EDCIMLA → ⬚⬚⬚⬚⬚⬚⬚

Solution on page 179

CROSSWORD

In this puzzle, write the answer to each clue in the crossword grid.
One letter goes into each square.

ACROSS

1) Adjust a camera lens
4) Style of speech
6) A big vase
7) Wild ox
9) Payment for an apartment
12) Red and white mixed
13) Shock someone
14) Roll out the red _____
15) A large fish
19) Can transport lots of people
20) Male child
21) A place to sleep
23) Where a king lives
25) Used to tie things
27) An explosive
28) Opposite of go
30) Word that goes with neither
32) Horizontally
35) A little wet
36) Very appealing
37) Put in a cup

DOWN

1) Two plus two
2) A metal piece of money
3) Our galaxy's star
4) Whichever
5) Was ripped
8) Particular space
10) Excited about
11) A home when camping
12) Salt and _____
14) A sweet treat
16) The two of ___
17) Opposite of yes
18) See them in the sky
22) A piece on a theatre stage
24) An industrious insect
26) A black and white bear
28) An emergency signal
29) Unusual
31) Talking in rhythm
32) Creative work
33) Kind of sleep
34) Be on a chair
35) Goes slightly lower

Solution on page 180

Starts with "K"

In this puzzle, the solution to each clue begins with the letter "K." You can write your answer in the blank space provided.

1. A sauce you might put on fries, eggs or a burger.

_____

2. A tap that lets someone know you would like to enter.

_____

3. Is often used with a fork or spoon during a meal.

_____

4. The concept that your actions come back to you in other forms.

_____

5. A tough cotton fabric than is often used for pants and uniforms.

_____

6. A marsupial that lives in Australia and surrounding islands.

_____

7. Is often used by kids going to school or people going on hike.

_____

8. Food for a pet that is dried and has small pieces.

_____

9. Information that people have learned and stored in their brains.

_____

10. The part of a door or drawer that lets people open it.

_____

11. Description used when a person is benevolent or considerate.

_____

12. A small barrel that can hold and sometimes dispense liquids.

_____

13. Use needles and yarn to create a garment or piece of fabric.

_____

14. Item that can unlock a door, car, or filing cabinet.

_____

15. An informal way to refer to people who live in New Zealand.

_____

16. A person who may move awkwardly or trip frequently.

_____

17. A small, light boat which uses a paddle with two blades.

_____

18. A healthy, dark green, or sometimes purple, leafy vegetable.

_____

Solution on page 180

Delightful Words

Try to create ten words from each group of letters. You do not need to use every letter in each word. However, you can only use the letters that are displayed once per word.

Letters	Letters	Letters
o a d n r s	e b i k t p	v e m c a s
Words	Words	Words

Solution on page 180

Clues & Rhymes
Swan and Sword

The answers to each clue in question one will rhyme with "swan." In question two, all of the answers will rhyme with "sword." You can put your answers on the blank lines provided.

QUESTION ONE: Answers Rhyme With "Swan."

A) Left or disappeared

_____

B) A baby deer

_____

C) Early morning

_____

D) A tired, deep inhale

_____

E) Strong muscles

_____

F) Piece in the game of chess

_____

QUESTION TWO: Answers Rhyme With "Sword."

A) A kind of rope

_____

B) A stash or collection

_____

C) Disinterested

_____

D) Overwhelmed, surprised

_____

E) Part of a hospital

_____

D) Put away

_____

Solution on page 180

WORD SEARCH
AN ADVENTURE

Find the words below in the letter grid to the right. Words may be hidden in an across, down, or diagonal direction. Also, the words may be spelled forwards or backwards.

WORD LIST:

SKYDIVING	UNUSUAL	TRIP
HIKE	EXTREME	REMOTE
TRAVEL	SAFARI	BOLD
EXPLORE	RISK	NEW
OCEAN	FUN	THREAT
CURIOSITY	VENTURE	QUEST
TREK	JOURNEY	DANGER
DIVE	HERO	EPIC
HAZARD	EXCITING	JUNGLE
OUTDOORS	ARTIFACT	TRAIL
RUSH	PERIL	CLIMB

```
R L Q M A E H C E B E T O M E R Q
L R A C A D Q D Z O E B H Z V S C
E X C I T I N G X K G R L K T K N
O B F P N S W H I P Q I U S T W O
X N M E F W F H O E C C N R E P P
C U R I O S I T Y R K A W N L W Q
E W A K C L X L L I E M E R T X E
Z N E D M F S W C L O F T P X F J
Z R W R C L R D E Y E R O L P X E
T P E A Q B O I T O G W C E O N Y
O A T Z U O O B A X E B H V V A F
R H R A E L D K E B K G J L Q I P
L L A H S D T Y R C L R N A N N D
I A I L T K U W H Y G U K I E K D
I U L B F E O W T N P S B B Y P T
R S H T R I P C I P D H K K J E R
A U H K K V A V H A C Z P I Z E A
F N W S Y F I I N L F V O S L L V
A U I G I D O G I R Y C Y D G G E
S R R T Y R E M Y E N R U O J N L
T T R K E R B V E N T U R E U U X
D A S H O C E A N A M H K F D J X
```

Solution on page 181

UNSCRAMBLE

TELEVISION

In this puzzle, the goal is to create words from the scrambled letters that relate to television and television shows. Every letter is used to make each word. Put one letter into each square.

1. GRROAMP → `p` `r` `o` `g` `r` `a` `m`

2. RREUN → `r` `e` `r` `u` `n`

3. AAMRD →

4. TAINGRS →

5. WNES → `n` `e` `w` `s`

6. VOEIM → `m` `o` `v` `i` `e`

7. UEBT → `t` `u` `b` `e`

8. AECBL → [ ][ ][ ][ ][ ]

9. WSOH → [ ][ ][ ][ ]

10. LCCIKRE → [ ][ ][ ][ ][ ][ ][ ]

11. WEOKTNR → [ ][ ][ ][ ][ ][ ][ ]

12. EOSIPDE → e p i s o d e

13. TSIOMC → [ ][ ][ ][ ][ ][ ]

14. ROSPTS → [ ][ ][ ][ ][ ][ ]

15. AOOTRCN → [ ][ ][ ][ ][ ][ ][ ]

16. EERSIS → [ ][ ][ ][ ][ ][ ]

17. NNCAHLE → [ ][ ][ ][ ][ ][ ][ ]

Solution on page 181

CROSSWORD

In this puzzle, write the answer to each clue in the crossword grid. One letter goes into each square.

ACROSS

1) Disappear
5) Vehicle that transports goods
8) Feel upbeat
10) Originally named
11) What's up _____?
13) A female deer
14) Day before a big day
15) Tree that comes from acorns
16) Value
20) Organ that detoxifies
21) Kind of stocking for women
23) Do, re, mi, fa, _____
24) A mind game
26) Soft part of a beach
28) Questions
30) Used to carry things
31) Goes fast on two legs
32) Hello
33) Cultured milk product
34) It fills up a lawn

DOWN

1) You catch more flies with honey than you do _____
2) Require
3) You put it on a foot
4) An exclamation when proven right
5) Particular kind of thing
6) Take apart
7) Knock with one's foot
9) Dessert with fruit
12) Food for horses
17) Sample of people's opinions
18) Makes something
19) Racket sport that can be played on grass and clay
22) A short sleep
24) Focused on unimportant things
25) A kind of beer
27) Puts under water
29) Glide over snow
30) Wet, spongy area

Solution on page 181

Starts with "O"

In this puzzle, the solution to each clue begins with the letter "O"
You can write your answer in the blank space provided.

1. A creature that lives in the ocean and has eight arms.

_____

2. It is both a tasty, tropical fruit and a color.

_____

3. A person that has neither a mother or a father.

_____

4. When something goes back and forth in a repetitive manner.

_____

5. What may given off by a flower, a rotten fish or a perfume.

_____

6. Completely unaware of what is going on or happening.

_____

7. It is part of the air we breath and is critical for humans.

_____

8. When a few people control the government or economy.

_____

9. A label for things that are outdated or no longer useful.

_____

10. A sign or symbol that indicates something will happen in the future.

_____

11. The shape of an elliptical race track or an egg.

_____

12. Follow another's directions or commands to the letter.

_____

13. They can be cold pressed to make a very healthy oil.

_____

14. If a person expresses their thoughts loudly and frankly.

_____

15. It is the likelihood or probability of something happening.

_____

16. A characteristic that means light can not go through.

_____

17. A black and white whale that is part of the dolphin family.

_____

18. A person or company's clearly stated goal or purpose.

_____

Solution on page 181

Delightful Words

Try to create ten words from each group of letters. You do not need to use every letter in each word. However, you can only use the letters that are displayed once per word.

Letters	Letters	Letters
h t u s n a	p w a e r l	y d m r a j
Words	**Words**	**Words**
_____	_____	_____
_____	_____	_____
_____	_____	_____
_____	_____	_____
_____	_____	_____
_____	_____	_____
_____	_____	_____
_____	_____	_____
_____	_____	_____
_____	_____	_____

Solution on page 182

Clues & Rhymes
Trade and Truck

The answers to each clue in question one will rhyme with "trade." In question two, all of the answers will rhyme with "truck." You can put your answers on the blank lines provided.

QUESTION ONE: Answers Rhyme With "Trade."

A) Moved back and forth
_____

B) Mark at school
_____

C) Had fun with a toy
_____

D) What trees provide
_____

E) Walk into water
_____

F) To dim or lose color
_____

QUESTION TWO: Answers Rhyme With "Truck."

A) Pull out
_____

B) Unable to get out
_____

C) A sound a hen makes
_____

D) Good fortune
_____

E) Mud and dirt
_____

F) A bird that swims
_____

Solution on page 182

WORD SEARCH
UNDERGROUND

Find the words below in the letter grid to the right. Words may be hidden in an across, down, or diagonal direction. Also, the words may be spelled forwards or backwards.

WORD LIST:

TUNNEL	BURROW	CAVE
SEWER	GOLD	MOLE
GRAVEL	WATER	CHALK
ANT	ROOTS	WIRES
FOSSILS	MINE	SOIL
ROCK	GRANITE	COAL
WOMBAT	WORM	SAND
CELLAR	FOOTING	HOLE
CLAY	SHALE	BUNKER
COPPER	PIPES	BADGER
SUBWAY	BASEMENT	DIAMONDS

```
J M I M J N X Q C V C C A V E F J
L P Y G R W I R S B S Q I G O S U
E Q F W C O V K S H A L E O T C M
N C E A B M Z R L U Z X T O B P Z
N H X T W B D N I H U I O A R R C
U A U E T A P X O K N R S F S D O
T L O R H T X U S G E E J D K I P
A K U G R R E W E S M A N G N I P
Y F P A V B A D G E R O O N X W E
W U P D L S D S N C M B X Y Q C R
S N M K R S L T X A B U R R O W A
E Y T B R O R I I U P J Y Z G E K
P B P D A I O D S W M P G O L D W
I W R A L L C S C S R J E O H Y I
P E O U L C K B K B O V M T A Q R
E E C G E O M H C Q W F F W Q R E
T L Z T C N A M N L R I B C Y N S
I O R N M J J M U E E U S K G M A
N H U A L D B I K Y S V Q T L R G
A N S R N X T N I Y A Z A C O A L
R A S A J J U E Z Y C L Y R M S R
G M S U R B Y O V N P B C R G X Q
```

Solution on page 182

UNSCRAMBLE
AT THE GYM

In this puzzle, the goal is to create words from the scrambled letters that relate to exercise and the gym. Every letter is used to make each word. Put one letter into each square.

1. OOWURKT →

2. TSTRCHE →

3. OAYG →

4. EIWGHST →

5. UUSPHP →

6. ITFSESN →

7. WTSAE →

8. RABBLLE → ⬜⬜⬜⬜⬜⬜⬜

9. ATM → ⬜⬜⬜

10. OCERKL → ⬜⬜⬜⬜⬜⬜

11. RANTIRE → ⬜⬜⬜⬜⬜⬜⬜

12. HCBNE → ⬜⬜⬜⬜⬜

13. ARCOID → ⬜⬜⬜⬜⬜⬜

14. OOTIMN → ⬜⬜⬜⬜⬜⬜

15. MUJP → ⬜⬜⬜⬜

16. URN → ⬜⬜⬜

17. LULPEY → ⬜⬜⬜⬜⬜⬜

Solution on page 182

CROSSWORD

In this puzzle, write the answer to each clue in the crossword grid. One letter goes into each square.

ACROSS

1) Strong wooden box
3) Leap into the air
5) Everything
7) Go into a room
10) Outer skin of an orange
12) River in South America
13) The Wizard of ___
14) Marry
15) Card game in Vegas
19) Rule made by a government
20) Chuckle
23) A mistake
26) A basketball league
27) Be courageous
28) Look at
29) ___ de Janeiro
30) Opposite of yes
32) Opposite of early
35) Pull behind a truck
36) Grand ___ Opry
37) Opposite of wild
38) Santa's helper

DOWN

1) Dust, wash, etc.
2) Bet place in poker
4) Silly decision maker
5) Sugar ___ spice
6) Upset
8) Used for shaving
9) Holds back water
11) Opposite of out
14) Healthy
15) Synthetic textile
16) Get ready
17) Place where animals can live and be observed
18) Used to remove hairs
21) Imaginary
22) She lays eggs
24) Do again
25) Repeat of a tv show
31) Night bird that hoots
33) ___ grapes of wrath
34) Be in debt to
36) ___ Mice and Men

Solution on page 183

Starts with "W"

In this puzzle, the solution to each clue begins with the letter "W."
You can write your answer in the blank space provided.

1. A person's collection of clothing for a season or a year.

_____

2. A written guarantee for a car, appliance or other item.

_____

3. A valuable combination of experience and knowledge.

_____

4. Exhausted or tired from work or another endeavor.

_____

5. Carefree, unpredictable, and predisposed to flights of fancy.

_____

6. Good fortune that is either sudden or unexpected.

_____

7. An enchanted person who may practice magic.

_____

8. A tool that is used for gripping or turning things.

_____

9. Intricate thread structure made by a spider to catch insects.

_____

10. Smart banter or a clever conversational ability.

_____

11. Word for something that is untamed or unpredictable.

_____

12. When a person moves at a regular pace by foot.

_____

13. A particularly large, bold lie or a fantastic, false story.

_____

14. When someone likes, needs or desires something.

_____

15. A popular breakfast food that is made with pancake batter.

_____

16. A soft, thin organism that has neither arms or legs.

_____

17. A question that tries to unearth a cause or reason.

_____

18. Greet another in a very friendly and inviting manner.

_____

Solution on page 183

Delightful Words

Try to create ten words from each group of letters. You do not need to use every letter in each word. However, you can only use the letters that are displayed once per word.

Letters	Letters	Letters
s t r e n i	y o n c d e	h s o t l a
Words	**Words**	**Words**
stein		
in		
tie		
rent		
ire		
tire		
ten		
rest		

Clues & Rhymes
COPE & CROW

The answers to each clue in question one will rhyme with "cope." In question two, all of the answers will rhyme with "crow." You can put your answers on the blank lines provided.

QUESTION ONE: Answers Rhyme With "Cope."

A) Used to wash something

Soap

B) A thick cord

rope

C) Brownish gray

_____

D) Incline of a hill

_____

E) Brood or sulk

_____

F) Optimistic expectation

_____

QUESTION TWO: Answers Rhyme With "Crow."

A) What the wind does

_____

B) Give off a bright light

_____

C) Understand

_____

D) Toss

_____

E) Move along

_____

F) Put away

_____

Solution on page 183

BRAIN STORM

Write down of all the different countries that you can name in two minutes. Can you think of thirty-two?

1. _____
2. _____
3. _____
4. _____
5. _____
6. _____
7. _____
8. _____
9. _____
10. _____
11. _____
12. _____
13. _____
14. _____
15. _____
16. _____
17. _____

18. _____
19. _____
20. _____
21. _____
22. _____
23. _____
24. _____
25. _____
26. _____
27. _____
28. _____
29. _____
30. _____
31. _____
32. _____
33. _____
32. _____

LOGIC
AND
NUMBER
BRAIN GAMES

- ✓ **DIVINE DEDUCTION**
- ✓ **TALLY TOTALS**
- ✓ **SOLVING THE SEQUENCE**
- ✓ **SUDOKU**
- ✓ **STEP BY STEP**
- ✓ **ODD NUMBER OUT**
- ✓ **IT'S ALL RELATIVE**
- ✓ **LOCATION, LOCATION**

DIVINE DEDUCTION
WHICH PAINTING?

This is a logic puzzle. Use the clues and grid provided to answer the question. Quick tip: when a clue or deductive reasoning rules out a possibility "x" out that spot in the grid.

THE SITUATION

Tom, Kim and George are friends who are taking an art class together. Each friend painted a different style of painting to display in the show that the class puts together at the end of their course. Use the clues below to determine which kind of painting each person created.

CLUES

1) Tom did not make the abstract painting.

2) Kim did not make the landscape painting.

3) George made either the abstract or landscape painting.

4) The portrait was made by either George or Kim.

Style	Tom	Kim	George
Abstract			
Portrait			
Landscape			

YOUR ANSWER

Tom: _____   Kim: _____   George: _____

Tally Totals
Garden Smarts

Use your math skills to solve question below. You can find the numbers you need in the clues. Quick tip: there are often numbers in the clues section that are not relevant to the question.

QUESTION

Terry's garden is being featured in a new lifestyle magazine. The journalist writing the magazine would like to know: How many shrubs and bushes does Terry has in her garden?

CLUES

- Terry has 42 boxwood bushes.
- Terry has 32 daffodils flowers.
- Terry has 12 burning bush shrubs.
- Terry has 2 maple trees.
- Terry has 6 gardenia shrubs.
- Terry also has a pond and a gazebo.

CALCULATION ZONE

YOUR ANSWER: _____

Solution on page 184

SOLVING THE SEQUENCE

In this puzzle, you are trying to identify the pattern in a given sequence. Write down the next three numbers, symbols, or letters of the pattern in the blank spaces provided.

SEQUENCE ONE

🌢 , ☺ , ☺ , 🌢 , ☺ , ☺ , 🌢 , ☺ , ☺ , ___ , ___ , ___

SEQUENCE TWO

● , ■ , ◆ , ● , ■ , ◆ , ● , ■ , ◆ , ___ , ___ , ___

SEQUENCE THREE

? , ! , ? , ? , ! , ? , ? , ! , ? , _?_ , ___ , ___

SEQUENCE FOUR

2 , 4 , 6 , 8 , 10 , 12 , 14 , 16 , 18 , 20 , 22 , 22

SEQUENCE FIVE

A , T , T , A , T , T , A , T , T , ___ , ___ , ___

SEQUENCE SIX

G , 1 , G , 2 , G , 1 , G , 2 , G , 1 , ___ , ___ , ___

Solution on page 184

SUDOKU

In this sudoku puzzle, you use the numbers 1 to 9 to fill in the grid. To finish the grid, you need to know three rules:

1. Every vertical row must have each of the numbers 1, 2, 3, 4, 5, 6, 7, 8 and 9 only once.

2. Every horizontal row must have each of the numbers 1, 2, 3, 4, 5, 6, 7, 8 and 9 only once.

3. Each square must have each of the numbers 1, 2, 3, 4, 5, 6, 7, 8 and 9 only once.

2	3	5	1	7		6	8	4
6		8	4	3				
1	4	7	6	8		9	2	3
4	1		3	9	7	2	5	8
	2		5		1	7		
	7	9	2		8	4	3	1
3	6	1				8	9	2
	4	9	2	3				6
9		2	8		6			7

Solution on page 184

STEP BY STEP

Follow the four steps below to decode this popular saying:

1. Replace all the 'X's with 'S's.
2. Replace all the 'B's with 'L's.
3. Replace all the 'T's with 'N's.
4. Replace all the 'A's with 'E's.

You can stop at any step, once you can decode the saying!

TO UXA CRYITG OVAR XPIBBAD MIBK.

 1. Replace the 'X's with 'S's.

_____

 2. Replace the 'B's with 'L's.

_____

 3. Replace the 'Ts with 'N's.

_____

 4. Replace the 'A's with 'E's.

_____

Solution on page 185

ODD NUMBER OUT

In this puzzle, you are looking for one number that is different in a meaningful way from all the other numbers.

PUZZLE ONE

2   4   14   102   18   102

90   32   46   61   38   10

60   88   6   8   24

76   62   12   84   52   84

PUZZLE TWO

5   20   90   95   65   105

200   32   85   250   110   10

60   155   15   65   70

75   80   305   45   85   40

-103-   Solution on page 185

IT'S ALL RELATIVE

In this puzzle, you use the tilt of the scale to help you determine the relative weight of each object. For example, if one side of the scale is lower than the other, it means that the items on the lower side are heavier than the items on the higher side.

QUESTION

Which of these three objects is the heaviest?

CLUES

ANSWER: _____

Location, Location

In this puzzle, use logical reasoning to determine the location of each person. The clues and diagram below will help you figure out the answer.

Question

Kelly, Sam, Jim and Sarah went to dinner on Friday night. Can you figure out where each person sat using the clues and diagram? You can write their names directly into the seating chart.

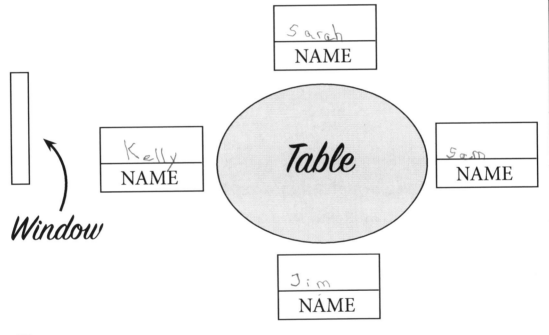

Sarah
NAME

Kelly
NAME

Table

Sam
NAME

Window

Jim
NAME

Clues

- Kelly sat right beside the window.
- Sarah sat beside Kelly and Sam.
- Sam sat furthest away from the window.
- Jim sat to Sam's left.

Solution on page 185

DIVINE DEDUCTION
BIRTHDAY CELEBRATION

This is a logic puzzle. Use the clues and grid provided to answer the question. Quick tip: when a clue or deductive reasoning rules out a possibility "x" out that spot on the grid.

QUESTION

Three friends are helping John celebrate his 60th birthday: June, Dan, and Christine. The group will all go out to dinner, and then each friend will give John a different gift: golf balls, a gift card, and a shirt. What gift is each friend planning to give John for his birthday?

CLUES

1) Christine will give John either the golf balls or the gift card.

2) Dan will not give John the golf balls.

3) June will not give John the shirt.

4) The golf balls will be given by either June or Dan.

Gift	June	Dan	Christine
Golf balls	√	X	X
Shirt	X		
Gift card			

YOUR ANSWER

June: _golf balls_ Dan: _____ Christine: _____

Tally Totals

Scrapbooking

Use your math skills to solve question below. You can find the numbers you need in the clues. Quick tip: there are often numbers in the clues section that are not relevant to the question.

QUESTION

Samantha is creating a scrapbook for her bowling club's tenth anniversary. Many club members have donated photographs. Samantha wants to include all of the donated pictures, so everyone feels included. How many pages will be in her scrapbook?

CLUES

- There are 120 donated pictures.
- Samantha can fit 4 picture on each page.
- There will be 4 extra pages (with no pictures) that include the title page and some extra information.
- Samantha will use 6 bottles of glue.
- She will also need 3 markers and 300 stickers.

CALCULATION ZONE

YOUR ANSWER: _____

Solution on page 185

SOLVING THE SEQUENCE

In this puzzle, you are trying to identify the pattern in a given sequence. Write down the next three numbers, symbols, or letters of the pattern in the blank spaces provided.

SEQUENCE ONE

3 , 4 , 7 , 8 , 11 , 12 15 , 16 , 19 , ___ , ___ , ___

SEQUENCE TWO

A , 1 , B , 2 , C , 3 , D , 4 , E , 5 , ___ , ___ , ___

SEQUENCE THREE

96 , 92 , 88 , 84 , 80 , 76 , 72 , 68 , 64 , ___ , ___ , ___

SEQUENCE FOUR

♦ , ♦ , ■ , ● , ♦ , ♦ , ■ , ● , ♦ , ___ , ___ , ___

SEQUENCE FIVE

1 , 2 , ● , 3 , 4 , ● , 5 , 6 , ● , ___ , ___ , ___

SEQUENCE SIX

3 , ■ , 6 , ■ , 9 , ■ , 12 , ■ , 15 , ■ , ___ , ___ , ___

Solution on page 186

SUDOKU

In this sudoku puzzle, you use the numbers 1 to 9 to fill in the grid. To finish the grid, you need to know three rules:

1. Every vertical row must have each of the numbers 1, 2, 3, 4, 5, 6, 7, 8 and 9 only once.

2. Every horizontal row must have each of the numbers 1, 2, 3, 4, 5, 6, 7, 8 and 9 only once.

3. Each square must have each of the numbers 1, 2, 3, 4, 5, 6, 7, 8 and 9 only once.

9	7	2	1	3		5		
3		5	8	6		2		4
	8	4			9	1		7
2	5		4	1	6		7	3
	9		3		8		5	2
7	3		9	2	5	4	8	1
5	2	3		8	1	7	4	
		7		9	2	3	1	
1		9	7		3	8		5

Solution on page 186

STEP BY STEP

Follow the four steps below to decode this popular saying:

1. Replace all the '**P**'s with '**L**'s.
2. Replace all the '**M**'s with '**T**'s.
3. Replace all the '**C**'s with '**G**'s.
4. Replace all the '**U**'s with '**I**'s.

You can stop at any step, once you can decode the saying!

APP MHAM CPUMMERS US NOM COPD.

 1. Replace the '**P**'s with '**L**'s.

 2. Replace the '**M**'s with '**T**'s.

 3. Replace the '**C**s with '**G**'s.

 4. Replace the '**U**'s with '**I**'s.

Solution on page 186

ODD NUMBER OUT

In this puzzle, you are looking for one number that is different in a meaningful way from all the other numbers.

PUZZLE ONE

8.1   6.3   5.4   9.2   4.4   1.1

9.4   4.2   3.1   8.7   3.4   8.1

6.9   7.8   6.2   11   7.2

7.6   6.2   1.2   8.4   5.2   3.1

PUZZLE TWO

3   63   32   39   53   103

75   113   303   230   123   43

63   153   13   34   93

39   73   203   37   83   35

Solution on page 186

IT'S ALL RELATIVE

In this puzzle, you use the tilt of the scale to help you determine the relative weight of each object. For example, if one side of the scale is lower than the other, it means that the items on the lower side are heavier than the items on the higher side.

QUESTION

Which of the following objects is the heaviest?

CLUES

YOUR ANSWER: _____

Solution on page 186

Location, Location

In this puzzle, use logical reasoning to determine the location of each family. The clues and diagram below will help you figure out the answer.

Question

Four families live on Oak Street, their last names are: Smith, Brown, Zehr, and Lewis. Where on Oak Street is each family located? You can write your answers directly on the diagram.

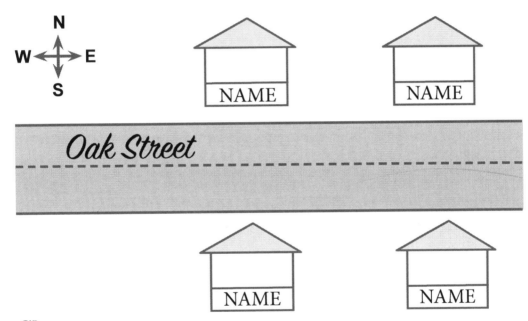

Clues

- The Brown family and Zehr family do not live on the north side of the street.
- The Smith family lives west of the Lewis family.
- The Zehr family do not live directly across the street from the Smith family.

Solution on page 186

DIVINE DEDUCTION
FLEA MARKET FINDS

This is a logic puzzle. Use the clues and grid provided to answer the question. Quick tip: when a clue or deductive reasoning rules out a possibility "x" out that spot on the grid.

QUESTION

Kelly, Fred and Sherry went to the local flea market together. They had a great time rummaging through all of the stalls and bargaining over prices. At the end of the day, each person found one item that they decided to purchase. Can you figure out which item each person bought?

CLUES

1) Fred did not purchase the vase.
2) Sherry bought either the chair or the vase.
3) Kelly did not purchase the chair.
4) The scarf was purchased by either Kelly or Sherry.

Item	Kelly	Fred	Sherry
Chair			
Scarf			
Vase			

YOUR ANSWER

Kelly: _____   Fred: _____   Sherry: _____

Tally Totals
Picnic Table

Use your math skills to solve question below. You can find the numbers you need in the clues. Quick tip: there may be numbers in the clues section that are not relevant to the question.

QUESTION

Larry and his grandson Patrick are going to build a picnic table. To do so, they will need 12 planks of wood, 200 nails, and a new saw. How much money will they need to get their supplies, so they can build their picnic table?

CLUES

- One plank of wood costs $8.00.
- Nails cost $2.00 for a box of 100.
- A small container of paint costs $5.00.
- A new hammer costs $9.00.
- A new saw costs $5.00.
- Screwdrivers are on sale for $1.99 for a box of 200.

CALCULATION ZONE

YOUR ANSWER: _____

Solution on page 187

SOLVING THE SEQUENCE

In this puzzle, you are trying to identify the pattern in a given sequence. Write down the next three numbers, symbols, or letters of the pattern in the blank spaces provided.

SEQUENCE ONE

72, 67, 62, 57, 52, 47, 42, 37, 32, ___, ___, ___

SEQUENCE TWO

Z, Y, 1, X, W, 2, V, U, 3, T, ___, ___, ___

SEQUENCE THREE

●, ◆, ●, ●, ◆, ●, ●, ◆, ●, ___, ___, ___

SEQUENCE FOUR

■, ◆, ■, ●, ■, ◆, ■, ●, ■, ___, ___, ___

SEQUENCE FIVE

3, 6, ●, 9, 12, ●, 15, 18, ●, ___, ___, ___

SEQUENCE SIX

?, !, 10, ?, !, 20, ?, !, 30, ___, ___, ___

Solution on page 187

SUDOKU

In this sudoku puzzle, you use the numbers 1 to 9 to fill in the grid. To finish the grid, you need to know three rules:

1. Every vertical row must have each of the numbers 1, 2, 3, 4, 5, 6, 7, 8 and 9 only once.

2. Every horizontal row must have each of the numbers 1, 2, 3, 4, 5, 6, 7, 8 and 9 only once.

3. Each square must have each of the numbers 1, 2, 3, 4, 5, 6, 7, 8 and 9 only once.

7	6	1	2	9	3	5	8	4
	3	8	4	5	7	1		9
5	4		6		8		3	2
1		7		4	5	6	9	8
3	8	6	7		9	4	5	1
		5		8	6		7	3
8		3	5	7	4	9	2	6
9	5					3	4	
	7	4	9	3	2	8	1	

Solution on page 187

STEP BY STEP

Follow the four steps below to decode the popular saying:

1. Replace all the 'B's with 'A's.
2. Replace all the 'Y's with 'O's.
3. Replace all the 'X's with 'S's.
4. Replace all the 'Q's with 'T's.

You can stop at any step, once you can decode the saying!

BCQIYNX XPEBK LYUDER QHBN WYRDX.

 1. Replace the 'B's with 'A's.

 2. Replace the 'Y's with 'O's.

 3. Replace the 'X's with 'S's.

 4. Replace the 'Q's with 'T's.

Solution on page 187

ODD NUMBER OUT

In this puzzle, you are looking for one number that is different in a meaningful way from all the other numbers.

PUZZLE ONE

4   72   8   68   64   16

56

44   76   24   76   60

80   52

40   88   72   86

84

20   36   32   28   48

PUZZLE TWO

102   999   323   812   748   602

451

235   751   303   230   123

789   931

631   153   170

140   250   48   230   831

435

    Solution on page 188

IT'S ALL RELATIVE

In this puzzle, you use the tilt of the scale to help you determine the relative weight of each object. For example, if one side of the scale is lower than the other, it means that the items on the lower side are heavier than the items on the higher side.

QUESTION

Which of the following objects is the lightest?

CLUES

YOUR ANSWER: _____

Location, Location

In this puzzle, use logical reasoning to determine the location of each farm. The clues and diagram below will help you figure out the answer.

Question

There are four farms located along the Speed River: Old MacDonald's Farm, Mary Milk Farm, Wild Wheat Farm and Peppy Peach Farm. What is the location of each farm? You can write your answer directly on the diagram.

Clues

- Peppy Peach Farm is located on the north side of the river.
- Mary Milk Farm is not on the same side of the river as Peppy Peach Farm.
- Wild Wheat Farm is located south of the speed river.
- Old MacDonald's Farm is east of Peppy Peach Farm.
- Mary Milk Farm is west of Wild Wheat Farm.

Solution on page 188

DIVINE DEDUCTION
POTLUCK

This is a logic puzzle. Use the clues and grid provided to answer the question. Quick tip: when a clue or deductive reasoning rules out a possibility "x" out that spot on the grid.

QUESTION

A group of friends are gathering a Joan's house for a potluck. Joan is preparing pizza as the main course. Her three helpful friends — John, James and Jill — will each bring in either cake, crackers or salad to help round out the meal. What dish will each person contribute to the potluck?

CLUES

1) John did not bring the cake.
2) James brought either the cake or the crackers.
3) Jill did not bring crackers.
4) The salad was brought by either James or John.

Item	John	James	Jill
Cake			
Salad			
Crackers			

YOUR ANSWER

John: _____   James: _____   Jill: _____

Tally Totals
Fitness Fun

Use your math skills to solve question below. You can find the numbers you need in the clues. Quick tip: sometimes there are numbers in the clues section that are not relevant to the question.

QUESTION

Sally is trying to burn more calories. To reach this goal, Sally plans to take the stairs instead of the elevator on Monday. Using the clues below, how many calories will Sally burn by taking the stairs on Monday?

CLUES

- Climbing the stairs to Sally's apartment uses 6 calories.
- Climbing down the stairs from Sally's apartment to the street uses 4 calories.
- Sally goes up and down the stairs to her apartment 8 times on Monday.

CALCULATION ZONE

YOUR ANSWER: _____

Solution on page 188

SOLVING THE SEQUENCE

In this puzzle, you are trying to identify the pattern in a given sequence. Write down the next three numbers, symbols, or letters of the pattern in the blank spaces provided.

SEQUENCE ONE

10, 5, 15, 10, 20, 15, 25, 20, 30, ___, ___, ___

SEQUENCE TWO

a, b, c, 1, d, e, f, 2, g, h, ___, ___, ___

SEQUENCE THREE

⬤, ◆, ■, ■, ⬤, ◆, ■, ■, ⬤, ___, ___, ___

SEQUENCE FOUR

90, 86, 82, 78, 74, 70, 66, 62, 58, ___, ___, ___

SEQUENCE FIVE

1, 8, ●, 15, 22, ●, 29, 36, ●, ___, ___, ___

SEQUENCE SIX

!, ?, -, -, !, ?, -, -, !, ?, ___, ___, ___

Solution on page 189

SUDOKU

In this sudoku puzzle, you use the numbers 1 to 9 to fill in the grid. To finish the grid, you need to know three rules:

1. Every vertical row must have each of the numbers 1, 2, 3, 4, 5, 6, 7, 8 and 9 only once.

2. Every horizontal row must have each of the numbers 1, 2, 3, 4, 5, 6, 7, 8 and 9 only once.

3. Each square must have each of the numbers 1, 2, 3, 4, 5, 6, 7, 8 and 9 only once.

	5	6	1	4	3	8	7	9
7		1	2	9	5			6
3	4	9	6	7	8			5
8	3		4	6	7	9		2
		7	9			4	3	
4	9	2			3	6	5	7
9	1	3	7	2	6	5		4
		4	3	8	9	7		1
		8	5	4	1	2	9	3

Solution on page 189

STEP BY STEP

Follow the four steps below to decode the popular saying:

1. Replace all the 'O's with 'E's.
2. Replace all the 'M's with 'T's.
3. Replace all the 'C's with 'G's.
4. Replace all the 'I's with 'S's.

You can stop at any step, once you can decode the saying!

MHO IQUOAKY WHOOL COMI MHO CROAIO.

 1. Replace the 'O's with 'E's.

 2. Replace the 'M's with **T**'s.

 3. Replace the 'Cs with 'G's.

 4. Replace the 'I's with 'S's.

Solution on page 189

ODD NUMBER OUT

In this puzzle, you are looking for one number that is different in a meaningful way from all the other numbers.

PUZZLE ONE

27   3   300   33   18   9

24   48   24   101   75   123

15   36   39   63   81   84

60   42   30   57   45   51

PUZZLE TWO

808   810   88   208   308   807

608   80   108   580   280   438

681   853   870   789   587

203   238   208   580   83   786

Solution on page 189

IT'S ALL RELATIVE

In this puzzle, you use the tilt of the scale to help you determine the relative weight of each object. For example, if one side of the scale is lower than the other, it means that the items on the lower side are heavier than the items on the higher side.

QUESTION

Which of the following objects is the heaviest?

CLUES

YOUR ANSWER: _____

Solution on page 189

Location, Location

In this puzzle, use logical reasoning to determine the location of each family. The clues and diagram below will help you figure out the answer.

Question

There are four sun umbrellas along the beach in front of the Happy Days Hotel. Each sun umbrella has been claimed by one the following families: Gelmans, Golds, Fords, and Firestones. Under which umbrella is each family located?

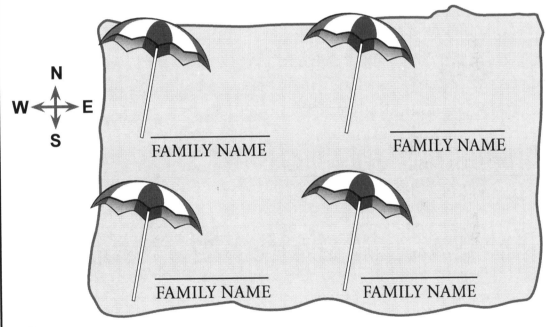

Clues

- The Gelmans and the Golds are on the north side of the beach.
- The Firestones are not on the west side of the beach.
- The Golds are directly north of the Fords on the beach.

Solution on page 189

DIVINE DEDUCTION
MARATHON

This is a logic puzzle. Use the clues and grid provided to answer the question. Quick tip: when a clue or deductive reasoning rules out a possibility "x" out that spot on the grid.

QUESTION

Three friends decided to train for a charity marathon together. After months of training Melvin, Mary, and Oscar successfully completed their marathon. Not only that, together they placed first, second and third. Can you figure out which place each friend came in the marathon?

CLUES

1) Melvin did not come in first.
2) Second went to either Mary or Oscar.
3) Oscar did not come third.
4) Mary did not come in first.

Item	Melvin	Mary	Oscar
First			
Second			
Third			

YOUR ANSWER

Melvin: _____   Mary: _____   Oscar: _____

Solution on page 190

Tally Totals
Craft Sale

Use your math skills to solve question below. You can find the numbers you need in the clues. Quick tip: sometimes there are numbers in the clues section that are not relevant to the question.

QUESTION

Janet is putting together a craft sale for local artists to share and sell their work. To do so, she is trying to determine how many tables she needs for the sale. Given the clues below, can you figure out how many tables Janet needs for the craft show?

CLUES

- There are 7 painters who are registered. Each painter will need one table each.
- There 24 quilters. Each quilter only needs to use half a table each.
- There are 6 potters, each of whom needs two tables each.

CALCULATION ZONE

YOUR ANSWER: _____

Solution on page 190

SOLVING THE SEQUENCE

In this puzzle, you are trying to identify the pattern in a given sequence. Write down the next three numbers, symbols, or letters of the pattern in the blank spaces provided.

SEQUENCE ONE

99, 90, 81, 72, 63, 54, 45, 36, 27, ____, ____, ____

SEQUENCE TWO

n, n, 10, o, o, 11, p, p, 12, ____, ____, ____

SEQUENCE THREE

🌢, 🌢, 6, 🌢, 🌢, 12, 🌢, 🌢, 18, ____, ____, ____

SEQUENCE FOUR

10, 6, 11, 7, 12, 8, 13, 9, 14, ____, ____, ____

SEQUENCE FIVE

0, 3, a, c, 6, 9, e, g, 12, ____, ____, ____

SEQUENCE SIX

&, %, %, $, &, %, %, $, &, %, ____, ____, ____

Solution on page 190

SUDOKU

In this sudoku puzzle, you use the numbers 1 to 9 to fill in the grid. To finish the grid, you need to know three rules:

1. Every vertical row must have each of the numbers 1, 2, 3, 4, 5, 6, 7, 8 and 9 only once.

2. Every horizontal row must have each of the numbers 1, 2, 3, 4, 5, 6, 7, 8 and 9 only once.

3. Each square must have each of the numbers 1, 2, 3, 4, 5, 6, 7, 8 and 9 only once.

5		1	8	7	3			4
8	2	3	1		4	7	5	
	7		5		9	8	1	3
1	8	7	2	3	5	4	9	6
3					7			8
6	5	2	4	9	8	3	7	1
2	1	4	3	5	6	9	8	7
		5	9			6		
9	6	8	7			1		

Solution on page 190

STEP BY STEP

Follow the four steps below to decode the popular saying:

1. Replace all the '**M**'s with '**A**'s.
2. Replace all the '**J**'s with '**E**'s.
3. Replace all the '**Y**'s with '**B**'s.
4. Replace all the '**Z**'s with '**R**'s.

You can stop at any step, once you can decode the saying!

YJTWJJN M ZOCK MND M HMZD PLMCJ.

 1. Replace the '**M**'s with '**A**'s.

 2. Replace the '**J**'s with **E**'s.

 3. Replace the '**Y**s with '**B**'s.

 4. Replace the '**Z**'s with '**R**'s.

Solution on page 190

ODD NUMBER OUT

In this puzzle, you are looking for one number that is different in a meaningful way from all the other numbers.

PUZZLE ONE

851   503   350   58   15   59

524   580   54   158   75   835

155   358   35   851   5   508

625   452   358   58   582   91

PUZZLE TWO

146   810   230   450   550   130

67   203   308   890   210   145

281   340   870   450   677

280   238   208   902   832   906

Solution on page 191

IT'S ALL RELATIVE

In this puzzle, you use the tilt of the scale to help you determine the relative weight of each object. For example, if one side of the scale is lower than the other, it means that the items on the lower side are heavier than the items on the higher side.

QUESTION

Which of the following objects is the lightest?

CLUES

YOUR ANSWER: _____

Solution on page 191

MEMORY
AND
TRIVIA
BRAIN GAMES

✓ **TRIVIA MATCHING**
✓ **LOVELY LISTS**
✓ **COMPLETE IT**
✓ **TERRIFIC TRIVIA CHALLENGES**

TRIVIA MATCHING
INVENTORS & INVENTIONS

In this trivia challenge, the goal is to match the person with the item that they are known for creating or discovering. You can draw a line to match items, or write your answers below.

NAME	INVENTION OR DISCOVERY
1. Alexander Graham Bell	A. Electric Light Bulb
2. Benjamin Franklin	B. Insulin
3. Thomas Edison	C. Morse Code
4. Alessandro Volta	D. Penicillin
5. Wright Brothers	E. Television
6. Tim Berners-Lee	F. Bifocals
7. Samuel Morse	G. Telephone
8. Alexander Fleming	H. World Wide Web
9. John Logie Baird	I. Powered Aircraft
10. Frederick Banting	J. Battery

ANSWERS:

1._____   2._____   3._____   4._____   5._____

6._____   7._____   8._____   9._____   10._____

Solution on page 191

Lovely Lists..... Shopping

In each puzzle, memorize the list and then turn the page and circle the words you remember in the word grid.

Tina's going shopping. To the right is the list of groceries she wants to buy. Once you think you've memorized the list turn the page.

Tina's Groceries

apples	beans
buns	flour
peppers	sugar

turn the page

Rob is going shopping. To the right is the list of hardware items he wants to buy. Once you think you've memorized the list turn the page.

Rob's List

nails	plaster
paint	hooks
hammer	screws

turn the page

These two puzzles are continued from the previous page.

Tina's Groceries

Circle the items that you remember from Tina's Grocery list in the word grid to the right.

from previous page

apples	banana	yogurt
chicken	orange	sugar
beans	ketchup	cereal
soup	lettuce	flour
radishes	spinach	salt
tomato	peppers	tofu
fish	cheese	buns

Rob's List

Circle the items that you remember from Rob's list in the word grid to the right.

from previous page

ladder	hammer	paint
saw	wrench	shovel
locks	glue	tape
tarp	nails	drill
screws	grout	wire
bolts	wood	plaster
hooks	knob	window

Solution on page 192

Complete It!
Common Sayings

In this trivia challenge, the goal is to fill in the missing word in these common sayings.

1. Two _wrong_ don't make a right.

2. When the going gets tough, the _toug_ get going.

3. Birds of a feather _____ together.

4. A chain is only as strong as its _____ link.

5. Money doesn't grow on _____.

6. Never look a _____ horse in the mouth.

7. A watched _pot_ never boils.

8. Too many _____ spoil the broth.

9. One man's _____ is another man's treasure.

10. Don't put all your _____ in one basket.

Solution on page 192

TERRIFIC TRIVIA CHALLENGE
LAND & WATER

In this trivia challenge, choose the answer to each question from one of the four options provided. If you do not know the answer, try to start by eliminating options that you know are wrong.

1. Which ocean can be found along the coast of Japan?
A. Atlantic   B. Pacific   C. Indian   D. Arctic

2. Which country does not border Brazil?
A. Bolivia   B. Columbia   C. Chili   D. Peru

3. In what country does the Nile River not flow through?
A. Egypt   B. Spain   C. Sudan   D. Uganda

4. Which of the following continents covers the largest area?
A. Asia   B. Australia   C. Europe   D. Africa

5. What mountain range is located in North America?
A. Rockies   B. Himalayas   C. Alps   D. Andes

6. What is the name of the largest lake in North America?
A. Erie   B. Ontario   C. Huron   D. Superior

7. Which country does not share a border with Austria?
A. Germany   B. Hungary   C. Poland   D. Italy

8. Which country has coastline along the Mediterranean Sea?
A. Mexico   B. Greece   C. Canada   D. Portugal

9. Which of the following deserts is located in the USA?
A. Mojave   B. Sahara   C. Kalahari   D. Gobi

10. Which river can be found in Australia?
A. Rhine   B. Murray   C. Amazon   D. Seine

11. What sea can be found off the coast of Sweden?
A. Celtic   B. Labrador   C. Black   D. Baltic

12. Which of the following is the world's tallest mountain?
A. Everest   B. K2   C. Makalu   D. Lhotse

13. Which of the following islands is the largest?
A. Iceland   B. Greenland   C. Cuba   D. Borneo

14. What is the longest river in the USA?
A. Mississippi   B. Yukon   C. Colorado   D. Missouri

15. Which of the following countries does not border Algeria?
A. Morocco   B. Libya   C. Tunisia   D. Venezuela

16. Which island can be found in the Caribbean Sea?
A. Jamaica   B. Macquarie   C. Fiji   D. Devon

17. Which country does not border China?
A. Nepal   B. Mongolia   C. Turkey   D. Vietnam

Solution on page 192

TRIVIA MATCHING
COUNTRIES & CAPITALS

In this trivia challenge, the goal is to match the country with their official capital city. You can draw a line to match items, or write your answers below.

COUNTRY	CAPITAL
1. Bahamas	A. Ottawa
2. USA	B. Berlin
3. Turkey	C. Stockholm
4. Peru	D. Nassau
5. Canada	E. Beijing
6. Sweden	F. Washington
7. New Zealand	G. Ankara
8. Germany	H. Havana
9. China	I. Wellington
10. Cuba	J. Lima

ANSWERS:

1._____   2._____   3._____   4._____   5._____

6._____   7._____   8._____   9._____   10._____

Solution on page 193

Lovely Lists..... Packing

In each puzzle, memorize the list and then turn the page and circle the words you remember in the word grid.

Sam's going on vacation. To the right is the list of items Sam has left to pack. Once you think you've memorized the list turn the page.

Sam's List

towel	brush
socks	money
shorts	phone

turn the page

Julie is going on a day trip. To the right is the list of items she wants to make sure she brings. Once you think you've memorized the list turn the page.

Julie's List

camera	juice
blanket	book
sandwich	hat

turn the page

These two puzzles are continued from the previous page.

Sam's List

Circle the items that you remember from Sam's packing list in the word grid to the right.

from previous page

towel	pen	shirts
sweater	socks	camera
soap	comb	shorts
shoes	brush	tie
money	vest	jacket
gel	razor	phone
pen	paper	book

Julie's List

Circle the items that you remember from Julie's list in the word grid to the right.

from previous page

water	camera	pop
juice	pizza	tv
sweater	book	pie
tent	pillow	blanket
sandwich	hat	ball
shovel	box	candy
cheese	crackers	map

Solution on page 193

Complete It!
Famous Quotations

In this trivia challenge, the goal is to fill in the missing word in these famous quotations.

1. "I _____ therefore I am." — *Rene Descartes*

2. "Hitch your wagon to a _____." — *Ralph Emerson*

3. "The _____ stops here." — *Harry Truman*

4. "To err is human, to forgive _____." — *Alexander Pope*

5. "What doesn't kill us makes us _____." — *Nietzsche*

6. "Be _____; everyone else is already taken." — *O. Wilde*

7. "There are lies, damned lies and _____" — *Mark Twain*

8. "May you live all the _____ of your life." — *Jonathan Swift*

9. "Turn your wounds into _____." — *Oprah Winfrey*

10. "Necessity is the mother of _____." — *Plato*

Solution on page 194

TERRIFIC TRIVIA CHALLENGE
HISTORY & POLITICS

In this trivia challenge, choose the answer to each question from one of the four options provided. Quick tip: if you do not know the answer, start by eliminating options that you know are wrong.

1. In what year did World War Two end?
A. 1944　　　B. 1945　　　C. 1955　　　D. 1919

2. Who was the first president of the United States?
A. Washington　　B. Adams　　C. Grant　　D. Adams

3. When did Jacques Chirac first become president of France?
A. 1965　　　B. 1975　　　C. 1985　　　D. 1995

4. What year did West Germany and East Germany reunify?
A. 1970　　　B. 1980　　　C. 1990　　　D. 2000

5. Who is Britain's longest serving British Monarch?
A. Elizabeth II　B. James VI　C. Victoria　D. David II

6. How long was Ronald Reagen president of the USA?
A. 2 years　　　B. 4 years　　　C. 6 years　　　D. 8 years

7. Who was the first prime minister of Canada?
A. MacDonald　B. Trudeau　C. Campbell　D. Clark

8. What year did World War One begin?
A. 1912   B. 1913   C. 1914   D. 1915

9. Which country is not part of the NATO Alliance?
A. Canada   B. Poland   C. Italy   D. Japan

10. What year did Napoleon's Battle of Waterloo occur?
A. 1815   B. 1825   C. 1835   D. 1845

11. What is the scandal that caused President Nixon to resign?
A. Iran Contra   B. Watergate   C. Lewinski   D. DR Blue

12. Which British prime minister was referred to as Iron Lady?
A. Major   B. May   C. Thatcher   D. Blair

13. What was the last state to join the United States?
A. Hawaii   B. Texas   C. Alaska   D. Arizona

14. Who was President of the United States after William Taft?
A. Truman   B. Clinton   C. Wilson   D. Ford

15. England had a "hundred years war" with whom?
A. Germany   B. France   C. Portugal   D. Spain

16. When did John Kennedy become President of the USA?
A. 1960   B. 1961   C. 1962   D. 1963

17. When was the Magna Carta adopted by England?
A. 1215   B. 1415   C. 1615   D. 1815

 Solution on page 194

TRIVIA MATCHING
AUTHORS & BOOKS

In this trivia challenge, the goal is to match the person with the book they are known for writing. You can draw a line to match items, or write your answers below.

NAME	BOOK
1. Charles Dickens	**A.** *Pride and Prejudice*
2. J. R. R. Tolkien	**B.** *The Catcher in the Rye*
3. Lewis Carroll	**C.** *To Kill a Mockingbird*
4. Dan Brown	**D.** *The Great Gatsby*
5. J. D. Salinger	**E.** *The Da Vinci Code*
6. Anna Sewell	**F.** *The Hobbit*
7. E.B. White	**G.** *A Tale of Two Cities*
8. Harper Lee	**H.** *Black Beauty*
9. F. Scott Fitzgerald	**I.** *Charlotte's Web*
10. Jane Austen	**J.** *Alice in Wonderland*

ANSWERS:

1. _____   2. _____   3. _____   4. _____   5. _____

6. _____   7. _____   8. _____   9. _____   10. _____

Solution on page 194

Lovely Lists..... Planning

In each puzzle, memorize the list and then turn the page and circle the words you remember in the word grid.

Karen is planning a party. To the right is a list of things she has left to purchase for the party. Once you think you've memorized the list turn the page.

Karen's List

balloons candy
gift pinata
cake napkins

turn the page

Bob is planning a fishing trip with his friends. To the right is a list of things he has to pack. Once you think you've memorized the list turn the page.

Bob's List

rod line
lures hat
worms gloves

turn the page

These two puzzles are continued from the previous page.

Karen's List

Circle the items that you remember from Karen's list in the word grid to the right.

from previous page

plates	piñata	tables
balloons	chairs	napkins
banner	bags	ice
glasses	soda	gift
cake	coffee	tea
trays	flowers	linen
coaster	candy	music

Bob's List

Circle the items that you remember from Bob's list in the word grid to the right.

from previous page

boots	shirt	boat
bags	lures	lamp
line	vest	gloves
hooks	worms	tent
rod	matches	hat
jacket	towel	net
cooler	map	camera

Solution on page 195

Complete It!
Popular Metaphors

In this trivia challenge, the goal is to fill in the missing word in these popular metaphors.

1. It is raining cats and _____.

2. Standing on the _____ of giants.

3. Letting the _____ out of the bag.

4. Easy as _____.

5. An _____ pound gorilla.

6. Blind as a _____.

7. Batten down the _____.

8. _____ is the music of the soul.

9. You are my _____.

10. A _____ of snow covered the ground.

Solution on page 195

TERRIFIC TRIVIA CHALLENGE
SPORTS & ATHLETICS

In this trivia challenge, choose the answer to each question from one of the four options provided. Quick tip: if you do not know the answer, start by eliminating options that you know are wrong.

1. In what sport did Olympian Michael Phelps compete in?
A. Running   B. Swimming   C. Golf   D. Tennis

2. What event is not part of the summer Olympic triathlon?
A. Swimming   B. Biking   C. Canoeing   D. Running

3. In what category did Olympian Carl Lewis compete in?
A. Track   B. Judo   C. Tennis   D. Rugby

4. Which tournament is not part of a tennis Grand Slam?
A. Wimbledon   C. Australian Open
B. French Open   D. European Open

5. How long is a traditional marathon?
A. 26.219 miles/ 42.195 km   C. 19.312 miles/ 31.07 km
B. 36.521 miles/ 58.7749 km   D. 42.14 miles/ 67.817 km

6. What sport is Derek Jeter well know for playing?
A. Cricket   B. Basketball   C. Football   D. Baseball

7. How many innings are there in a regular Major League Baseball game if there is no overtime?

A. 8   B. 9   C. 10   D. 11

8. In what sport did Jack Nicklaus excel in?

A. Football   B. Baseball   C. Golf   D. Tennis

9. In what country was soccer (football) player Cristiano Ronaldo born in?

A. Portugal   B. Spain   C. England   D. Brazil

10. Which athlete scored the first perfect score in gymnastics at the Olympic games?

A. Mary Lou Retton   C. Mo Huilan

B. Gaby Douglas   D. Nadia Comaneci

11. Which famous hockey player is known as 'The Great One'?

A. Bobby Orr   C. Gordie Howe

B. Wayne Gretzky   D. Mario Lemieux

12. What is the official height of the hoop for the National Basketball Association?

A. 9 feet/ 2.743 meters   C. 10 feet/ 3.048 meters

B. 11 feet/ 3.352 meters   D. 12 feet/ 3.657 meters

13. What is the color of the jersey that is worn by the leader of the Tour de France bicycling competition?

A. Green   B. Yellow   C. Red   D. Blue

Solution on page 195

TRIVIA MATCHING
LANGUAGE & HOW TO SAY HELLO

In this trivia challenge, the goal is to match the language with how you can say hello in that language. You can draw a line to match items, or write your answers below.

LANGUAGE	HOW TO SAY HELLO
1. Japanese	**A.** Namaste
2. German	**B.** Hola
3. Hindi	**C.** Aloha
4. Spanish	**D.** Dobrý den
5. Italian	**E.** Konnichiwa
6. Mandarin	**F.** Bonjour
7. Hawaiian	**G.** Goededag
8. Czech	**H.** Ni Hau
9. French	**I.** Ciao
10. Dutch	**J.** Guten tag

ANSWERS:

1. _____   2. _____   3. _____   4. _____   5. _____

6. _____   7. _____   8. _____   9. _____   10. _____

Solution on page 196

Lovely Lists..... Lottery

In each puzzle, memorize the list of numbers and then turn the page and circle the numbers you remember in the number grid.

Charlie likes to play the lottery. In particular, he has six lucky numbers, listed on the right, that he always plays. Once you think you've memorized his list turn the page.

Charlie's Numbers

3	91
43	10
8	2

turn the page

Beth likes to play the lottery. In particular, she has six lucky numbers, listed on the right, that she always plays. Once you think you've memorized her list turn the page.

Beth's Numbers

9	72
33	4
6	22

turn the page

These two puzzles are continued from the previous page.

Charlie's Numbers

Circle the numbers that you remember from Charlie's list in the number grid to the right.

from previous page ➡

5	15	8
91	87	7
101	102	2
72	10	63
43	86	90
5	3	15
62	67	80

Beth's Numbers

Circle the numbers that you remember from Beth's list in the number grid to the right.

from previous page ➡

8	9	18
21	11	4
33	87	97
62	38	39
49	6	87
40	42	22
72	74	28

Solution on page 196

Complete It!
Expressions & Idioms

In this trivia challenge, the goal is to fill in the missing word in these popular expressions and idioms.

1. A penny for your _____.

2. Don't count your _____ before the eggs have hatched.

3. Cross that _____ when you come to it.

4. Give the _____ of the doubt.

5. Your guess is as good as _____.

6. Best thing since _____ bread.

7. Between a rock and a _____ place.

8. Get up on the wrong side of the _____.

9. The bigger they are the harder they _____.

10. Up a _____ without a paddle.

Solution on page 197

TERRIFIC TRIVIA CHALLENGE
STARS & SPACE

In this trivia challenge, choose the answer to each question from one of the four options provided. Quick tip: if you do not know the answer, start by eliminating options that you know are wrong.

1. What is the name for the astrological sign for people who are born between May 21st and June 20th?

A. Taurus   B. Gemini   C. Cancer   D. Aries

2. What planet is closest to the sun?

A. Mercury   B. Venus   C. Earth   D. Jupiter

3. How does Earth's moon effect the oceans?

A. Coral   B. Color   C. Heat   D. Tides

4. In which galaxy is earth located?

A. Andromeda   B. Milky Way   C. Centaurus   D. GN-z11

5. What plant has visible rings around it?

A. Pluto   B. Venus   C. Jupiter   D. Saturn

6. How often is Halley's Comet visible from earth?

A. 74–79 years   C. 45-49 years
B. 104-109 years   D. 209-220 years

7. What was the name of the first artificial satellite?
A. Rosetta B. Sputnik 1 C. InSight D. Explorer

8. What the main source of energy for stars?
A. Hydroelectric C. Shale oil
B. Geothermal D. Nuclear fusion

9. What was the name of the United States' first space station that orbited earth?
A. Skylab B. Bluezone C. Challenger D. Stardust

10. What star constellation has the shape of a lion?
A. Aquarius B. Leo C. Libra D. Orion

11. Who was the first astronaut to set foot on the moon?
A. Buzz Aldrin C. Neil Armstrong
B. James Irwin D. David R. Scott

12. What do you call a place in outer space that is dark because the force of gravity does not let light escape?
A. Black Hole B. Black Dot C. Dwarf Star D. Red Giant

13. Which astronomer is celebrated for proposing that the earth is not the center of the universe?
A. Herschel B. Halley C. Sagan D. Copernicus

14. Which planet was demoted to dwarf planet status in 2006?
A. Jupiter B. Pluto C. Venus D. Mars

 Solution on page 197

TRIVIA MATCHING
ACTOR & MOVIE

In this trivia challenge, the goal is to match the actor with the movie in which they starred. You can draw a line to match items, or write your answers below.

ACTOR		MOVIE	
1.	John Wayne	A.	*Top Gun*
2.	Meryl Streep	B.	*Lawrence of Arabia*
3.	Clark Gable	C.	*The Godfather*
4.	Tom Cruise	D.	*Cool Hand Luke*
5.	Elizabeth Taylor	E.	*True Grit*
6.	Leonardo DiCaprio	F.	*Gone with the Wind*
7.	Marlon Brando	G.	*Titanic*
8.	Audrey Hepburn	H.	*Breakfast at Tiffany's*
9.	Paul Newman	I.	*Cleopatra*
10.	Peter O'Toole	J.	*Sophie's Choice*

ANSWERS:

1. _____   2. _____   3. _____   4. _____   5. _____

6. _____   7. _____   8. _____   9. _____   10. _____

Solution on page 197

Lovely Lists..... To Do

In each puzzle, memorize the list and then turn the page and circle the words you remember in the word grid.

Trish likes to garden. In particular, she has a list of things she wants to do in her garden today. Once you think you've memorized her list turn the page.

Trish's List

rake   water
plant   prune
fertilize   weed

turn the page

Ben likes to work on home maintenance. In particular, he has a list of things he wants to check this week. Once you think you've memorized his list turn the page.

Ben's List

gutters   lawn
windows   vents
deck   pump

turn the page

These two puzzles are continued from the previous page.

Trish's List

Circle the tasks that you remember from Trish's list in the word grid to the right.

from previous page →

shovel	rake	spray
mow	pick	plant
fertilize	hoe	tidy
paint	crop	water
prune	clean	seed
netting	compost	harvest
clear	weed	dig

Ben's List

Circle the tasks that you remember from Ben's list in the word grid to the right.

from previous page →

gutters	lawn	door
driveway	siding	fence
windows	heater	vents
deck	faucets	drains
toilet	pump	roof
lights	railings	fans
chimney	filters	paint

Solution on page 198

Complete It!
Movie Titles

In this trivia challenge, the goal is to fill in the missing word in these famous movie titles.

1. *One Flew Over the* _____ *Nest*

2. *The Good, the Bad and the* _____

3. *Harry Potter and the* _____ *Hallows*

4. *Mr. Smith Goes to* _____

5. *Who's Afraid of* _____ *Woolf?*

6. *The* _____ *of Robin Hood*

7. *Butch Cassidy and the* _____ *Kid*

8. *Raiders of the Lost* _____

9. *A Streetcar Named* _____

10. *A* _____ *Without a Cause*

Solution on page 198

TERRIFIC TRIVIA CHALLENGE
PLENTY OF PLANTS

In this trivia challenge, choose the answer to each question from one of the four options provided. Quick tip: if you do not know the answer, start by eliminating options that you know are wrong.

1. What do you call flowers that can grow for many years?
A. Annuals   B. Perennials   C. Biennials   D. Growials

2. Which of the following is an evergreen tree?
A. Spruce   B. Maple   C. Oak   D. Birch

3. What is the official flower of the United States?
A. Orchid   B. Trillium   C. Daisy   D. Rose

4. Which flower's bulb provided the basis for financial speculation and crisis in Holland in 1637?
A. Caladium   B. Tulip   C. Daffodil   D. Lily

5. Generally, which is the tallest growing tree in the world?
A. Redwood   B. Ash trees   C. Beeches   D. Elms

6. Which expression is used with respect to a good gardener?
A. Forest feet   C. Green thumb
B. Leafy head   D. Earthy eyes

7. What is the name of the green pigment found in leaves?
A. Xylem   B. Synthesis   C. Chlorophyll   D. Jade

8. Which of the following is a product of a palm tree?
A. Lemon   B. Coconut   C. Kiwi   D. Apple

9. What is the fastest growing wooded plant?
A. Bamboo   B. Willow   C. Ceder   D. Beech

10. What is the name of the Japanese art of growing and pruning small trees in pots?
A. Topiary   B. Sculpture   C. Bonsai   D. Sushi

11. Which vegetable does not grow below the ground?
A. Carrot   B. Potato   C. Beet   D. Spinach

12. Which kind of tree does not produce cones?
A. Spruce   B. Oak   C. Pine   D. Juniper

13. Which of the following insects or animals does not act as a pollinator for flowers?
A. Honey bees   C. Humming birds
B. Bats   D. Worms

14. Which tree has white bark?
A. Aspen   B. Hickory   C. Hemlock   D. Cedar

15. To be considered a fruit, what must the item contain?
A. Sweetness   B. Seeds   C. Juice   D. Husk

Solution on page 198

TRIVIA MATCHING
COUNTRY & CURRENCY

In this trivia challenge, the goal is to match the country with the kind of money or currency that is used in that country. You can draw a line to match items, or write your answers below.

COUNTRY	CURRENCY
1. France	**A.** Pound
2. China	**B.** Won
3. India	**C.** Rupee
4. Iceland	**D.** Euro
5. United States	**E.** Króna
6. Mexico	**F.** Dollar
7. Russia	**G.** Yuan
8. South Korea	**H.** Yen
9. Japan	**I.** Ruble
10. England	**J.** Peso

ANSWERS:

1. _____   2. _____   3. _____   4. _____   5. _____

6. _____   7. _____   8. _____   9. _____   10. _____

SOLUTIONS

Page 8: Maze

Page 9: Spot Odd One Out

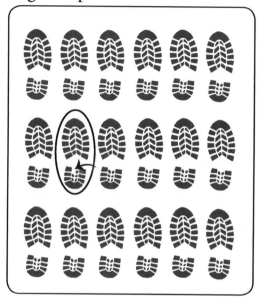

Page 10: 5 Differences

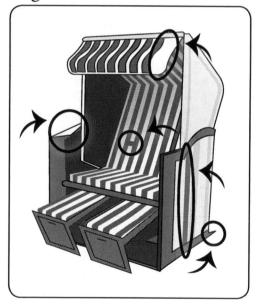

Page 11: Shadow Finder

Page 12: Pictures to Sayings

1) Read between the lines.
2) Put your best foot forward.

Page 13: Arrangements

1) Wet behind the ears.
2) Ace in the hole.

Page 14: Maze

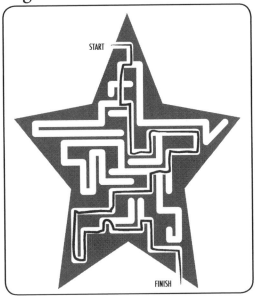

Page 15: Spot Odd One Out

Page 16: 5 Differences

Page 17: Shadow Finder

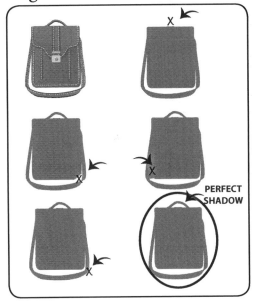

Page 18: Pictures to Sayings

1) The pen is mightier than the sword.
2) Cool as a cucumber.

Page 19: Arrangements

1) Foot in the door.
2) Wrong end of the stick.

Page 20: Maze

Page 21: Spot Odd One Out

Page 22: 5 Differences

Page 23: Shadow Finder

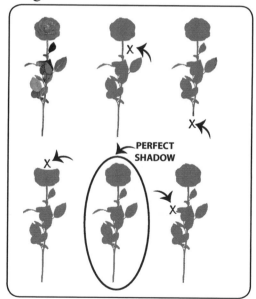

Page 24: Picture to Sayings

1) A picture is worth a thousand words.
2) Think outside the box.

Page 25: Arrangements

1) Fall from grace.
2) Head over heels.

Page 26: Maze

Page 27: Spot Odd One Out

Page 28: 5 Differences

Page 29: Shadow Finder

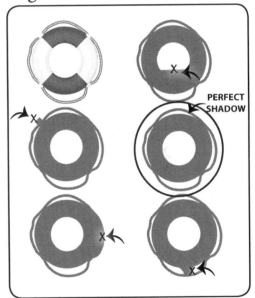

Page 30: Picture to Sayings

1) Put the cart before the horse.
2) Money can't buy happiness.

Page 31: Arrangements

1) Sit on the fence.
2) A drop in the bucket.

Page 32: Maze

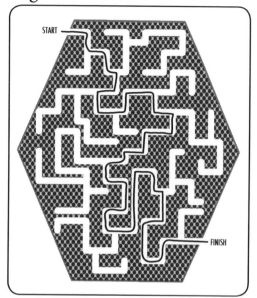

Page 33: Spot Odd One Out

Page 34: 5 Differences

Page 35: Shadow Finder

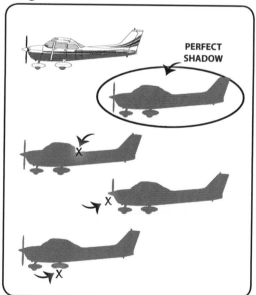

Page 36: Picture to Sayings

1) An apple a day keeps the doctor a way.
2) Two heads are better than one.

Page 37: Arrangements

1) Hot off the press.
2) Jump on the bandwagon.

Page 38: Maze

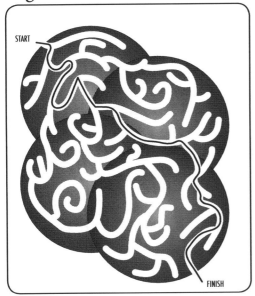

Page 39: Spot Odd One Out

Page 40: 5 Differences

Page 41: Shadow Finder

Page 42: Picture to Sayings

1) The buck stops here.
2) Wear your heart on your sleeve.

Page 43: Arrangements

1) The writing on the wall.
2) Nip in the bud.

Page 44: Maze

End of Visual Puzzle and Brain Game Solutions

***

Start of Word Puzzle and Brain Game Solutions

Pages 46-47: Coffee or Tea

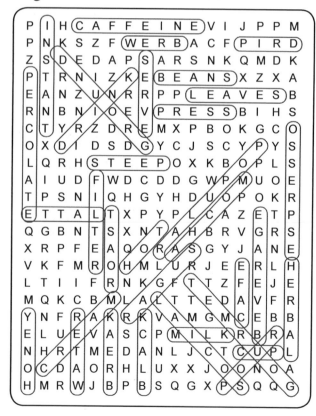

Pages 48-49: Newspapers

1. column
2. editor
3. byline
4. paper
5. local
6. advice
7. news
8. comics
9. reader
10. publish
11. inform
12. sports
13. ads
14. feature
15. review
16. story
17. article

Pages 50-51: Crossword

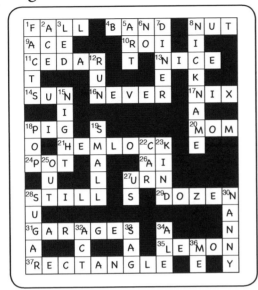

Pages 52-53: Starts with 'P'

1. potluck
2. parachute
3. pencil
4. piano
5. peacock
6. pasture
7. pebbles
8. prohibit
9. pickle
10. plumper
11. pillow
12. physics
13. penguin
14. pundit
15. pyramid
16. pancreas
17. prepare
18. pineapple

Page 54: Delightful Arrangements

Letters:
U N S L B A

Possible Words:
ab, abs, an, ban, bun, lab, nab, sun, sub, snub, slab, a, sub, us

Letters:
I T G F O Z

Possible Words:
fig, fit, zit, fog, gift, gif, git, go, got, if, it, of, to, tog

Letters:
Y R C A E M

Possible Words:
creamy, cream, mercy, car, race, acme, may, ray, year, rye, race, mare, a, ace, mace, are

Page 55: Quote & Quit

1) Rhymes with "Quote"			2) Rhymes with "Quit"		
A. tote	B. float	C. goat	A. knit	B. bit	C. kit
D. bloat	E. coat	F. wrote	D. mitt	E. slit	F. split

Pages 56-57: Symphony

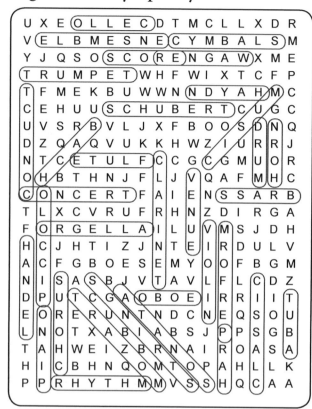

Pages 58-59: Wild Weather

1.	thunder	12.	cloudy
2.	gale	13.	sleet
3.	freeze	14.	tornado
4.	hail	15.	gust
5.	cyclone	16.	drought
6.	storm	17.	monsoon
7.	flood		
8.	snow		
9.	typhoon		
10.	squall		
11.	humidex		

Pages 60-61: Crossword

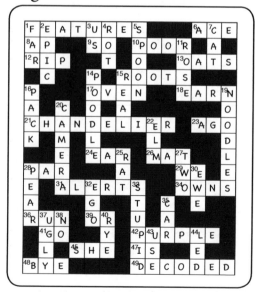

Pages 62-63: Starts with 'U'

1.	umbrella	11.	updo
2.	undertow	12.	unify
3.	universe	13.	uplift
4.	update	14.	unique
5.	umpire	15.	upstairs
6.	urgent	16.	urban
7.	usher	17.	utopia
8.	utensil	18.	unison
9.	unicorn		
10.	useless		

Page 64: Delightful Arrangements

Letters: PTUVAR	**Letters:** CGOWTE	**Letters:** JLNAES
Possible Words: part, rapt, tarp, trap, vat, put, par, apt, rap tap, put, art, tar, up	**Possible Words:** cow, cog, owe, two, tow, ego, toe, get, got wet, go, cot, to, woe	**Possible Words:** jeans, jean, lean, leans, sane, seal, sale, lane, a, an, sea, leas, lens, ale, as

Page 65: Free & Found

1) Rhymes with " Free"	**2) Rhymes with " Found"**
A. tea B. tree C. bee	A. hound B. sound C. pound
D. spree E. pea F. fee	D. ground E. round F. mound

Pages 66-67: Science Fiction

Pages 68-69: Mathematics

1. add	15. median
2. percent	16. graph
3. sum	17. decimal
4. number	
5. algebra	
6. angle	
7. integer	
8. formula	
9. ratio	
10. divide	
11. bracket	
12. zero	
13. factor	
14. average	

Pages 70-71: Crossword

Pages 72-73: Starts with 'K'

1. ketchup
2. knock
3. knife
4. karma
5. khaki
6. kangaroo
7. knapsack
8. kibble
9. knowledge
10. knob
11. kind
12. keg
13. knit
14. key
15. kiwi
16. klutz
17. kayak
18. kale

Page 74: Delightful Arrangements

Letters:
O A D N R S
Possible Words:
ad, ado, no, so, ados, an, and, do, arson, a, on, darn, nod, oar, adorn, radon, ran, road, sand

Letters:
E B I K T P
Possible Words:
be, bet, bike, bit, bite, it, kept, kip, kit, kite, pet, tie, tip, I, pit, pi, pie, pike

Letters:
V E M C A S
Possible Words:
ace, aces, acme, am, a, cam, came, case, cave, ma, mac, mace, mesa, scam, seam, vac, vase, as

Page 75: Swan & Sword

1) Rhymes with "Swan"
A. gone   B. fawn   C. dawn
D. yawn   E. brawn   F. pawn

2) Rhymes with "Sword"
A. cord   B. hoard   C. bored
D. floored   E. ward   F. stored

Pages 76-77: An Adventure

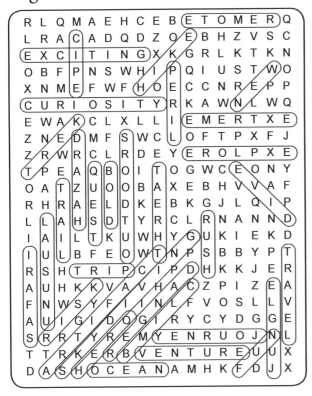

Pages 78-79: Television

1. program	15. cartoon
2. rerun	16. series
3. drama	17. channel
4. ratings	
5. news	
6. movie	
7. tube	
8. cable	
9. show	
10. clicker	
11. network	
12. episode	
13. sitcom	
14. sports	

Pages 80-81: Crossword

Pages 82-83: Starts with 'O'

1. octopus	11. oval
2. orange	12. obey
3. orphan	13. olives
4. oscillates	14. outspoken
5. odor	15. odds
6. oblivious	16. opaque
7. oxygen	17. orca
8. oligarchy	18. objective
9. obsolete	
10. omen	

Page 84: Delightful Arrangements

Letters:	**Letters:**	**Letters:**
H T U S N A	P W A E R L	Y D M R A J
Possible Words:	**Possible Words:**	**Possible Words:**
ash, at, aunt, has, hat, haunt, hut, nut, sat, shun, shut, stun, tan, than, thus, us, tuna, sun	ale, ape, are, ear, awe, lap, law, leap, pale, par, paw, pea, pew, wear pearls, rap, real, war, warp	ad, am, arm, a, army, dam, day, dry, jam, mad, may, ram, yard, yam, ray, rad, jay, jar, may

Page 85: Trade & Truck

1) Rhymes with "Trade"	**2) Rhymes with Truck**
A. swayed B. grade C. played	A. pluck B. stuck C. cluck
D. shade E. wade F. fade	D. luck E. muck F. duck

Pages 86-87: Underground

Pages 88-89: At the Gym

1. workout	15. jump
2. stretch	16. run
3. yoga	17. pulley
4. weights	
5. pushup	
6. fitness	
7. sweat	
8. barbell	
9. mat	
10. locker	
11. trainer	
12. bench	
13. cardio	
14. motion	

Pages 90-91: Crossword

Pages 92-93: Starts with 'W'

1. wardrobe
2. warranty
3. wisdom
4. weary
5. whimsical
6. windfall
7. wizard
8. wrench
9. web
10. wit
11. wild
12. walk
13. whopper
14. want
15. waffle
16. worm
17. why
18. welcome

Page 94: Delightful Arrangements

Letters:
S T R E N I

Possible Words:
inert, insert, is, it, its, nest, nets, nit, rein, rent, resin, resit, rest, ret, rin, rinse, risen, rite, sent, set, sin, siren, sit, site, stern

Letters:
Y O N C D E

Possible Words:
cod, code, coed, con, cone, coy, deco, den, deny, do, doc, doe, don, doyen, done, dye, eco, end, no, node, ode, on

Letters:
H S O T L A

Possible Words:
also, alt, alto, as, ash, at, halo, has, hat, hot, hosta, host, hot, lash, last, lat, loath, lost, lot, oat, oath, oats, salt, sat, shot, slat, slot, sloth, to

Page 95: Cope & Crow

1) Rhymes with "Cope"			2) Rhymes with "Crow"		
A. soap	B. rope	C. taupe	A. blow	B. glow	C. know
D. slope	E. mope	F. hope	D. throw	E. flow	F. stow

End of Word Puzzle and Brain Game Solutions

***

Start of Logic and Number Puzzle Solutions

Page 98: Divine Deduction, Which Painting?

Style	Tom	Kim	George
Abstract	X	X	✓
Portrait	X	✓	X
Landscape	✓	X	X

Tom: Landscape
Kim: Portrait
George: Abstract

Page 99: Tally Totals, Garden Smarts

Total shrubs and bushes = 42 boxwood bushes + 12 burning bush shrubs + 6 gardenia shrubs
= 60 shrubs and bushes

Page 100: Solving the Sequence

SEQUENCE ONE   ♦ , ☺ , ☺

SEQUENCE TWO   ● , ■ , ◆

SEQUENCE THREE   ? , ! , ?

SEQUENCE FOUR   20 , 22 , 24

SEQUENCE FIVE   A , T , T

SEQUENCE SIX   G , 2 , G

Page 101: Sudoku

2	3	5	1	7	9	6	8	4
6	9	8	4	3	2	1	7	5
1	4	7	6	8	5	9	2	3
4	1	6	3	9	7	2	5	8
8	2	3	5	4	1	7	6	9
5	7	9	2	6	8	4	3	1
3	6	1	7	5	4	8	9	2
7	8	4	9	2	3	5	1	6
9	5	2	8	1	6	3	4	7

Page 102: Step by Step

Phrase:

"NO USE CRYING OVER SPILLED MILK."

Page 103: Odd Number Out

PUZZLE ONE: 61, because it is the only odd number

PUZZLE TWO: 32, it is the only number not divisible by 5.

Page 104: It's All Relative

The gray square is the heaviest.

Page 105: Location, Location

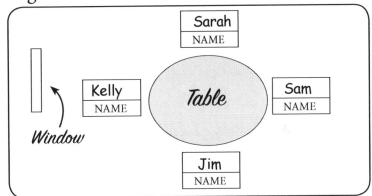

Page 106: Divine Deduction, Birthday Celebration

Style	June	Dan	Christine
Golf balls	✓	X	X
Shirt	X	✓	X
Gift card	X	X	✓

June: Golf Balls
Dan: Shirt
Christine: Gift Card

Page 107: Tally Totals, Scrapbooking

Number of pages for photos = 120 photos / 4 photos per page
= 30 pages

Total number of pages = 30 pages + 4 extra pages
= 34 pages

Page 108: Solving the Sequence

SEQUENCE ONE	**20 , 23 , 24**
SEQUENCE TWO	**F , 6 , G**
SEQUENCE THREE	**60 , 56 , 52**

SEQUENCE FOUR	◆ , ■ , ●
SEQUENCE FIVE	**7 , 8 , ●**
SEQUENCE SIX	18 , ■ , 21

Page 109: Sudoku

9	7	2	1	3	**4**	5	**6**	**8**
3	**1**	5	8	6	**7**	2	**9**	4
6	8	4	**2**	**5**	9	1	**3**	7
2	5	**8**	4	1	6	**9**	7	3
4	9	**1**	3	**7**	8	**6**	5	2
7	3	**6**	9	2	5	4	8	1
5	2	3	**6**	8	1	7	4	**9**
8	**4**	7	**5**	9	2	3	1	**6**
1	**6**	9	7	**4**	3	8	**2**	5

Page 110: Step by Step

Phrase:

"ALL THAT GLITTERS
IS NOT GOLD."

Page 111: Odd Number Out

PUZZLE ONE: 11, because it is the only number without a decimal.

PUZZLE TWO: 75, because it is the only number without the number 3 in it.

Page 112: It's All Relative

The patterned rectangle is the heaviest.

Page 113: Location, Location

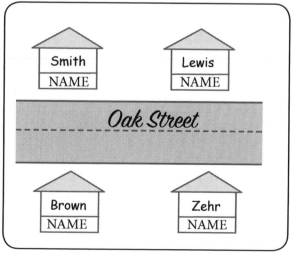

Page 114: Divine Deduction, Flea Market Finds

Style	Kelly	Fred	Sherry
Chair	X	✓	X
Scarf	✓	X	X
Vase	X	X	✓

Kelly: Scarf
Fred: Chair
Sherry: Vase

Page 115: Tally Totals, Picnic Table

Cost of wood = $8.00*12 = $96.00
Cost of nails = $2.00*2 = $4.00
Cost of a saw = $5.00

Total = $96.00 + $4.00 + $5.00
= $105.00
Cost of supplies is $105.00

Page 116: Solving the Sequence

SEQUENCE ONE	27, 22, 17	SEQUENCE FOUR	◆, ■, ●
SEQUENCE TWO	S, 4, R	SEQUENCE FIVE	21, 24, ●
SEQUENCE THREE	●, ◆, ●	SEQUENCE SIX	?, !, 40

Page 117: Sudoku

7	6	1	2	9	3	5	8	4
2	3	8	4	5	7	1	**6**	9
5	4	**9**	6	**1**	8	**7**	3	2
1	**2**	7	**3**	4	5	6	9	8
3	8	6	7	**2**	9	4	5	1
4	**9**	5	**1**	8	6	**2**	7	3
8	**1**	3	5	7	4	9	2	6
9	5	**2**	**8**	**6**	**1**	3	4	**7**
6	7	4	9	3	2	8	1	**5**

Page 118: Step by Step

Phrase:

"ACTIONS SPEAK LOUDER THAN WORDS."

Page 119: Odd Number Out

PUZZLE ONE: 86 , all numbers are divisible by 4 except 86

PUZZLE TWO: 48, all the other numbers have 3 digits

Page 120: It's All Relative

The patterned hexagon is the lightest.

Page 121: Location, Location

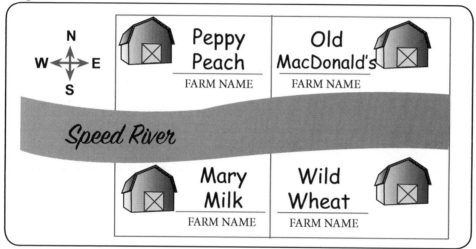

Page 122: Divine Deduction, Potluck

Item	John	James	Jill
Cake	X	X	✓
Salad	✓	X	X
Crackers	X	✓	X

John: Salad
James: Crackers
Jill: Cake

Page 123: Tally Totals, Fitness Fun

Calories up = 6 calories per set *8 set of stairs
              = 48 calories

Calories down = 4 calories per set * 8 set of stairs
              = 32 calories

Total calories = 48 calories +32 calories = 80 calories

Page 124: Solving the Sequence

SEQUENCE ONE	**25 , 35 , 30**
SEQUENCE TWO	**i , 3 , j**
SEQUENCE THREE	**◆ , ■ , ■**

SEQUENCE FOUR	**54 , 50 , 46**
SEQUENCE FIVE	**43 , 50 , ●**
SEQUENCE SIX	**- , - , !**

Page 125: Sudoku

2	5	6	1	3	4	8	7	9
7	8	1	2	9	5	3	4	6
3	4	9	6	7	8	1	2	5
8	3	5	4	6	7	9	1	2
1	6	7	9	5	2	4	3	8
4	9	2	8	1	3	6	5	7
9	1	3	7	2	6	5	8	4
5	2	4	3	8	9	7	6	1
6	7	8	5	4	1	2	9	3

Page 126: Step by Step

Phrase:

"THE SQUEAKY WHEEL GETS THE GREASE."

Page 127: Odd Number Out

PUZZLE ONE: 101, all the numbers are divisible by 3 except 101.

PUZZLE TWO: 203, all the numbers have an 8 in it, except 203.

Page 128: It's All Relative

The shaded double circle shape is the heaviest.

Page 129: Location, Location

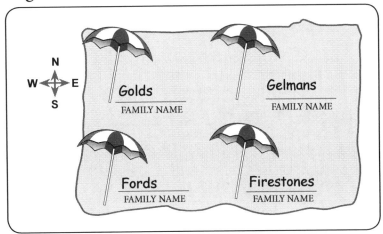

Page 130: Divine Deduction, Marathon

Item	Melvin	Mary	Oscar
First	X	X	✓
Second	X	✓	X
Third	✓	X	X

Melvin: Third
Mary: Second
Oscar: First

Page 131: Tally Totals, Craft Sale

Painters = 7 tables x 1 table each = 7 tables

Quilters = 24 quilters x 1/2 each = 12 tables

Potters = 6 potters x 2 tables each =12 tables

Total tables need = 7 tables + 12 tables +12 tables = 31 tables

Page 132: Solving the Sequences

SEQUENCE ONE	18 , 9 , 0	SEQUENCE FOUR	10 , 15 , 11
SEQUENCE TWO	q , q , 13	SEQUENCE FIVE	15 , i , k
SEQUENCE THREE	♦ , ♦ , 24	SEQUENCE SIX	% , $, &

Page 133: Sudoku

5	**9**	1	8	7	3	**2**	**6**	4
8	2	3	1	**6**	4	7	5	**9**
4	7	**6**	5	**2**	9	8	1	3
1	8	7	2	3	5	4	9	6
3	**4**	**9**	**6**	**1**	7	**5**	**2**	8
6	5	2	4	9	8	3	7	1
2	1	4	3	5	6	9	8	7
7	**3**	5	9	**8**	**1**	6	**4**	**2**
9	6	8	7	**4**	**2**	1	**3**	**5**

Page 134: Step By Step

Phrase:

"BETWEEN A ROCK AND A HARD PLACE."

Page 135: Odd Number Out

PUZZLE ONE: 91, only number without an 5 in it.
PUZZLE TWO: 67, all the numbers have three digits except 67.

Page 136: It's All Relative

The dotted circle is the lightest.

End of Logic & Number Puzzle Solutions

***

Start of Memory Games and Trivia Challenge Solutions

Page 138: Trivia Matching, Inventors & Inventions

1.	Alexander Graham Bell	→	**G.**	Telephone
2.	Benjamin Franklin	→	**F.**	Bifocals
3.	Thomas Edison	→	**A.**	Electric Light Bulb
4.	Alessandro Volta	→	**J.**	Battery
5.	Wright Brothers	→	**E.**	Powered Aircraft
6.	Tim Berners-Lee	→	**H.**	World Wide Web
7.	Samuel Morse	→	**C.**	Morse Code
8.	Alexander Fleming	→	**B.**	Penicillin
9.	John Logie Baird	→	**E.**	Television
10.	Frederick Banting	→	**B.**	Insulin

Page 139: Tina's Groceries

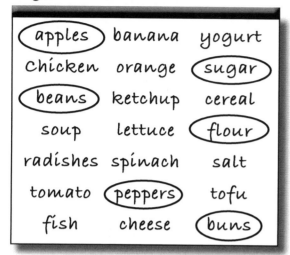

Page 139: Rob's List

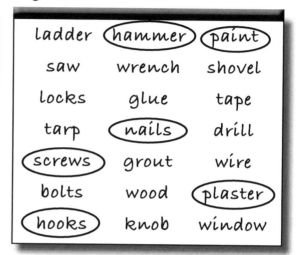

Page 141: Common Sayings

1. Two **wrongs** don't make a right.
2. When the going gets though, the **tough** get going.
3. Bird of a feather **flock** together.
4. A chain is only as strong as its **weakest** link.
5. Money doesn't grow on **trees**.
6. Never look a **gift** horse in the mouth.
7. A watched **pot** never boils.
8. Too many **cooks** spoil the broth.
9. One man's **trash** is another man's treasure.
10. Don't put all your **eggs** in one basket.

Pages 141-2: Terrific Trivia

1. *Option* B. Pacific
2. *Option* C. Chili
3. *Option* B. Spain
4. *Option* A. Asia
5. *Option* A. Rockies
6. *Option* D. Superior
7. *Option* C. Poland
8. *Option* B. Greece
9. *Option* A. Mojave
10. *Option* B. Murray
11. *Option* D. Baltic
12. *Option* A. Everest
13. *Option* B. Greenland
14. Option D. Missouri
15. *Option* D. Venezuela
16. *Option* A. Jamaica
17. *Option* C. Turkey

Page 144: Trivia Matching, Countries & Capitals

	COUNTRY			CAPITAL
1.	Bahamas	→	D.	Nassau
2.	USA	→	F.	Washington
3.	Turkey	→	G.	Ankara
4.	Peru	→	J.	Lima
5.	Canada	→	A.	Ottawa
6.	Sweden	→	C.	Stockholm
7.	New Zealand	→	I.	Wellington
8.	Germany	→	B.	Berlin
9.	China	→	E.	Beijing
10.	Cuba	→	H.	Havana

Page 146: Sam's List

towel   pen   shirts
sweater   socks   camera
soap   comb   shorts
shoes   brush   tie
money   vest   jacket
gel   razor   phone
pen   paper   book

Page 146: Julie's List

water   camera   pop
juice   pizza   tv
sweater   book   pie
tent   pillow   blanket
sandwich   hat   ball
shovel   box   candy
cheese   crackers   map

Page 147: Famous Quotations

1. "I **think** therefore I am."
2. "Hitch your wagon to a **star.**"
3. "The **buck** stops here." —
4. "To err is human, to forgive **divine**."
5. "What doesn't kill us makes us **stronger**."
6. "Be **yourself**; everyone else is already taken."
7. "There are lies, damned lies and **statistics**."
8. "May you live all the **days** of your life."
9. "Turn your **wounds** into wisdom."
10. "Necessity is the mother of **invention**."

Pages 148-9: History

1. *Option* B. 1945
2. *Option* A. Washington
3. *Option* D. 1995
4. *Option* C. 1990
5. *Option* A. Elizabeth II
6. *Option* D, 8 years
7. *Option* A. MacDonald
8. *Option* C. 1914
9. *Option* D. Japan
10. *Option* A. 1815
11. *Option* B. Watergate
12. *Option* C. Thatcher
13. *Option* A. Hawaii
14. *Option* C. Wilson
15 *Option* B. France
16 *Option* B. 1961
17. *Option* A. 1215

Page 150: Author & Books

1.	Charles Dickens	→ **G.**	*A Tale of Two Cities*
2.	J. R. R. Tolkien	→ **F.**	*The Hobbit*
3.	Lewis Carroll	→ **J.**	*Alice in Wonderland*
4.	Dan Brown	→ **E.**	*The Da Vinci Code*
5.	J. D. Salinger	→ **B.**	*The Catcher in the Rye*
6.	Anna Sewell	→ **H.**	*Black Beauty*
7.	E.B. White	→ **I.**	*Charlotte's Web*
8.	Harper Lee	→ **C.**	*To Kill a Mockingbird*
9.	F. Scott Fitzgerald	→ **D.**	*The Great Gatsby*
10.	Jane Austen	→ **A.**	*Pride and Prejudice*

Page 152: Karen's List

plates (pinata) tables
(balloons) chairs (napkins)
banner bags ice
glasses soda (gift)
(cake) coffee tea
trays flowers linen
coaster (candy) music

Page 152: Bob's List

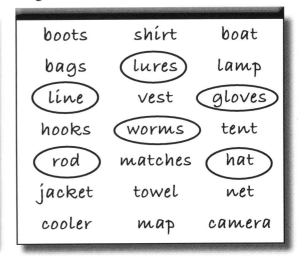

boots shirt boat
bags (lures) lamp
(line) vest (gloves)
hooks (worms) tent
(rod) matches (hat)
jacket towel net
cooler map camera

Page 153: Metaphors

1. It is raining **cats** and dogs.
2. Standing on the **shoulders** of giants.
3. Letting the **cat** of the bag.
4. Easy as **pie**.
5. An **eight hundred** pound gorilla.
6. As blind as a **bat**.
7. Batten down the **hatches**.
8. **Laughter** is the music of the soul.
9. You are my **sunshine**.
10. A **blanket** of snow covered the ground.

Pages 154-5: Sport & Athletics

1. *Option* B. swimming
2. *Option* C. canoeing
3. *Option* A. track
4. *Option* D. European Open
5. *Option* A. 26.219 miles/ 42.195 km
6. *Option* D. baseball
7. *Option* B. 9
8. *Option* C. golf
9. *Option* A. Portugal
10. *Option* D. Nadia Comaneci
11. *Option* B. Wayne Gretzky
12. *Option* C. 10 feet/ 3.048 meters
13. *Option* B. yellow

Page 156: Trivia Matching, Language & How To Say Hello

	LANGUAGE			HOW TO SAY HELLO
1.	Japanese	→	E.	Konnichiwa
2.	German	→	J.	Guten tag
3.	Hindi	→	A.	Namaste
4.	Spanish	→	B.	Hola
5.	Italian	→	I.	Ciao
6.	Mandarin	→	H.	Ni Hau
7.	Hawaiian	→	C.	Aloha
8.	Czech	→	D.	Dobrý den
9.	French	→	F.	Bonjour
10.	Dutch	→	G.	Goedendag

Page 158: Charlie's Numbers

5	15	(8)
(91)	87	7
101	102	(2)
72	(10)	63
(43)	86	90
5	(3)	15
62	67	80

Page 158: Beth's Numbers

8	(9)	18
21	11	(4)
(33)	87	97
62	38	39
49	(6)	87
40	42	(22)
(72)	74	28

Page 159: Expressions and Idioms

1. A penny for your **thoughts**.
2. Don't count your **chickens** before the eggs have hatched.
3. Cross that **bridge** when you come to it.
4. Give the **benefit** of the doubt.
5. Your guess is as good as **mine**.
6. Best thing since **sliced** bread.
7. Between a rock and a **hard** place.
8. Get up on the wrong side of the **bed**.
9. The bigger they are the harder they **fall**.
10. Up a **creek** without a paddle.

Pages 160-1: Stars & Space

1. *Option* B. Gemini
2. *Option* A. Mercury
3. *Option* D. Tides
4. *Option* B. Milky Way
5. *Option* D. Saturn
6. *Option* A. 74-79 years
7. *Option* B. Sputnik 1
8. *Option* D. Nuclear fusion
9. *Option* A. Skylab
10. *Option* B. Leo
11. *Option* C. Neil Armstrong
12. *Option* A. Black Hole
13. *Option* D. Copernicus
14. *Option* B. Pluto

Page 162: Trivia Matching, Actor & Movie

1. John Wayne → **E.** *True Grit*
2. Meryl Streep → **J.** *Sophie's Choice*
3. Clark Gable → **F.** *Gone With the Wind*
4. Tom Cruise → **A.** *Top Gun*
5. Elizabeth Taylor → **I.** *Cleopatra*
6. Leonardo DiCaprio → **G.** *Titanic*
7. Marlon Brando → **C.** *The Godfather*
8. Audrey Hepburn → **H.** *Breakfast at Tiffany's*
9. Paul Newman → **D.** *Cool Hand Luke*
10. Peter O'Toole → **B.** *Lawrence of Arabia*

Page 164: Trish's List

shovel · (rake) · spray
mow · pick · (plant)
(fertilize) · hoe · tidy
paint · crop · (water)
(prune) · clean · seed
netting · compost · harvest
clear · (weed) · dig

Page 164: Ben's List

(gutters) · (lawn) · door
driveway · siding · fence
(windows) · heater · (vents)
(deck) · faucets · drains
toilet · (pump) · roof
lights · railings · fans
chimney · filters · paint

Page 165: Movie Titles

1. One Flew Over the **Cuckoo's** Nest
2. The Good, the Bad, and the **Ugly**
3. Harry Potter and the **Deathly** Hallows
4. Mr. Smith Goes to **Washington**
5. Who's Afraid of **Virgina** Woolf?
6. The **Adventures** of Robin Hood
7. Butch Cassidy and the **Sundance** Kid
8. Raiders of the Lost **Ark**
9. A Streetcar Named **Desire**
10. A **Rebel** Without a Cause

Pages 166-7: Plenty of Plants

1. *Option* B. Perennials
2. *Option* A. Spruce
3. *Option* D. Rose
4. *Option* B. Tulip
5. *Option* A. Redwood
6. *Option* C. Green Thumb
7. *Option* C. Chlorophyll
8. *Option* B. Coconut
9. *Option* A. Bamboo
10. *Option* C. Bonsai
11. *Option* D. Spinach
12 *Option* B. Oak
13. *Option* D. Worms
14. *Option* A. Aspen
15. *Option* B. Seeds

Page 168: Trivia Matching, Country & Currency

1.	France	→	**D.**	Euro
2.	China	→	**G.**	Yuan
3.	India	→	**C.**	Rupee
4.	Iceland	→	**E.**	Króna
5.	United States	→	**F.**	Dollar
6.	Mexico	→	**J.**	Peso
7.	Russia	→	**I.**	Ruble
8.	South Korea	→	**B.**	Won
9.	Japan	→	**H.**	Yen
10.	England	→	**A.**	Pound

***

End of Solutions

THE END